Articles of WAR:

A REVOLUTIONARY CATECHISM

by WILLIAM BOOTH

& STEPHEN COURT

foreword by JIM KNAGGS

CREST BOOKS

Articles of War: *A Revolutionary Catechism*

Published by Crest Books

Crest Books
The Salvation Army National Headquarters
615 Slaters Lane
Alexandria, VA 22313
Phone: 703/684-5523

Lt. Col. Allen Satterlee, Editor-in-Chief and National Literary Secretary
Roger Selvage, Art Director
Jessica Curtis, Editorial Assistant

Available in print from crestbooks.com and in ebook form from wphstore.com

ISBN: 978-1-946709-03-5

Printed in the United States

Endorsements

Articles of War: A Revolutionary Catechism is a boon to Salvationist soldier-makers and disciplers. But this is not a regimen for the faint of heart, the comfortably Christian, the occasional Salvationist. This is for would-be warriors, for Cross-bearing holy militants who mean business about the Salvation War. Let the reader be prepared to sign on to a whole new level of covenantal commitment. It's what the Founder, on whose 1903 *Doctrines of The Salvation Army* this commentary is based, expected of his soldiers. It is what our cross-bearing, death-defying Savior still calls us to.

The endnotes are not to be missed.
Mine them for pure gold.

General Paul A. Rader (Ret.)

Articles of War: A Revolutionary Catechism is a unique and very important work, co-authored by William Booth and Stephen Court. It is about the covenant relationship all true Salvationists must have with God and the Army if we are to fulfill our purpose as part of the Body of Christ today. Steve uses a fascinating Question & Answer format, underpinning his clear and uncompromising answers with Scripture and leaving the reader with the inescapable responsibility to fill in some of the blanks. This is a must read and study source for all recruits and seasoned Salvationists. It can change the future.

Commissioner Robert Watson

Well written, comprehensive, creative and most enlightening. I wish this work had been available during my struggling corps officer days, and also during the administrative leadership years that followed, because I would have most certainly recommended this *Revolutionary Catechism* to those under my command. Kudos to Steve Court for this important undertaking which I predict will become an invaluable resource for corps officers, soldiers and recruits alike in the days to come.

Commissioner Joe Noland

For modern day Salvos this is a powerful text. It brings our heritage out of the dust and cobwebs of officious rhetoric and grounds it in the act of daily living. You won't necessarily agree with all of Court's assertions and interpretations—I don't. However, that is not the point with a text like this. It challenges, offends, rebukes and inspires—critical fuel for the fire of holiness that burns within us.

CSM Phil Wall

The book is certainly a forthright expression of radical conservatism which will evoke a fervent "Amen" in many quarters. At a time when some would urge a lowering of the bar it raises the standard high for the Lord.

Commissioner Wesley Harris

Articles of War: A Revolutionary Catechism stirs us to become all that we were intended to be: a covenanted people characterized by sacrifice and simplicity, being set-apart and disciplined, loyal citizens, having received revelation from our great God.

Questions that we would ask on key issues are answered with clarity, depth, and are easy to understand, and then the wrestle begins. Agree or disagree, but wrestle it well.

A challenge for us, in a world that needs us to be on our knees, rising up and moving forward, with the same call still in our lives. Urgent and exciting days require a covenanted people to take hold of all that God has for us, and all that He requires from us.

Lieutenant-Colonel Miriam Gluyas

Articles of War: A Revolutionary Catechism is a powerful blending of the theology, ethics, and missional passion of two soul mates, William Booth and Stephen Court. It is the expansion and updating of a doctrinal catechism and strategic plan for the salvation of the world first put forth by William Booth in 1903. As a catechism it is strewn with basic biblical teaching and penetrating questions calling for the Salvationist's response and action. It has no use for arm-chair theology, woolly thinking, or compromised conclusions. It follows Booth's principle of clarity, forcefulness, and usefulness. Incredibly straightforward, it brims with practical realism about what it takes actually to live in the world as a disciple of Jesus. Among the many attractive descriptions of the Christian life is the emphasis on the centrality of love (benevolence) in the character and living of the Christian. Among the uncomfortable facts is the absolute rejection of cheap forgiveness. The reader doesn't have to agree with every detail of the book's strategy to be affected and mobilized by the authors' call to turn everything over to Jesus and his Kingdom.

Commissioner Phil Needham

Booth and Court team up to help Salvationists rediscover the hidden gem of mission effectiveness - covenant. Love lived-out is a force for change both internally and externally. I believe this book could reawaken The Salvation Army to its radical roots of love. And I believe that this love story is one the world desperately needs.

Major Danielle Strickland

Wake up Tribe of Fire! It's time for us to embrace our militant, aggressive, surrendered, uncompromised calling as The Salvation Army in order to win the world for Jesus. Court invites us to come along with him as he re-digs Booth's salvation wells in both thought and practice. This book offers life giving springs to refresh and revive a weary and parched army. This revolutionary catechism reintroduces us to our tribal DNA and challenges us as a community to not only embrace but celebrate and effectively execute our militant calling. This is a must read and discuss book for all soldiers and recruits.

Captain Ruth Gillingham

Dedication

To the War Room in Vancouver and the authentic Christian community that feeds it and feeds off it.

Table of Contents

Part 2: The Declarations

Part 3: The Declarations

Acknowledgements

Thanks to Tara Ayer for transcribing the original 1903 William Booth text and to Captain Evelyn Clark for editing the newer text. Thanks for the generous comments of those who endorse the book. Thanks to Lt. Colonel Allen Satterlee and the team at CREST Publications for taking on the project. The manuscript also benefited from constructive comment by General Shaw Clifton, The War College, Lt. Colonel Laurie Robertson, Lt. Colonel Ray Moulton, Carla Evans, Captain Heather Dolby, Major Amy Reardon, Colonel Henry Gariepy, Revolution Hawaii, Major Danielle Strickland, Captain Genevieve Peterson, Major Wayne Ennis, Lieut-Colonel Peter Farthing, Major Peter McGuigan, Evangeline Court, and Wallace Court. The **Reading Club Guide** was improved by the contributions of Jonathan Evans. Thanks to Strickland, Harris, Campbell, White, Munn-Shirsath, Burrows, Gariepy, Webb and Castle, Coleman, Munn, Noland, Knaggs, Thompson, and Brookshaw – esteemed co-authors… Hallelujah.

Foreword

I know my way around covenants. I was a junior soldier. I became a senior soldier. I married my wonderful wife Carolyn. I signed my life away to God as an officer more than 40 years ago.

And I've been privileged to watch thousands of people enter these relationships with God. Covenant is a powerful thing.

Some people think that we make too much of covenants in our movement. And there certainly is a danger that legalists – and we have all been at least tempted that way at some point in our lives – wield a covenant like a cudgel to bludgeon people into conformity.

But I want to suggest to you that we, most of us, anyway, might actually under-rate covenant. We – some of us – signed up as junior soldiers because the cultural swarm was swooshing in that direction. Similarly, senior soldiership, too often after too brief training sessions, followed as a perfunctory rite of passage or, even worse, a hoop to jump through to qualify to play or sing in one of the music sections.

The Articles of War – a soldier's covenant – that every senior soldier in the world has signed, 1,056,722 of us currently, has nothing to do with the legalist or the perfunctory. Properly understood and wholeheartedly embraced, it is an incendiary document with historic, nay, even eternal ramifications.

There are two parts to the Articles of War: the beliefs and the declarations. General William Booth produced a catechistic primer more than a century ago for cadets that covered the beliefs portion of the covenant. And Major Stephen Court has crafted, more than a century later, a catechistic primer for all Salvationists on the declarations portion.

We continue to look to the Founder for inspiration and the purity of the Salvation mission. His indisputable focus and foundational faith must be told and retold. Using a current vernacular and placing it in contemporary context, Major Stephen Court does it again in his disciplined and dynamic manner to the glory of God and the advancement of The Salvation Army. Together they rescue the covenant from mis-understanding and misapplication and create Articles of War: A Revolutionary Catechism.

This book was a long time coming – not only with the timespan between co-author birthdays but in the development of the manuscript, but it is well worth the wait.

What emerges on every page is that this is all about God – loving God and God helping us love others effectually. Jesus has inspired the covenants I've made in my life and He has inspired the words on these pages. I'm convinced that they will inspire you in your love for the Lord Jesus Christ and through that love your love for others. Read it and live it.

Jim Knaggs
Commissioner (Rtd)

New Jersey - 2017

Introduction

Q. What in the world is this all about?

A. There have been wars and rumors of wars in eastern Europe, the Middle East, central Africa, and beyond – gun battles tallying death tolls each day. There are more complex spiritual struggles happening over religion and power and hedonism and relativism and lifestyle in your neighborhood right now.

Life with Christ is not merely a personal decision or relationship. Our purpose is not to be nice or helpful or pleasant. The Salvation Army Articles of War are a revolutionary document meant to put reins on zeal and engage with the greater culture in a transformative manner. We're meant to make a difference in our world. That's what this is all about.

Q. Why write a book called Articles of War: A Revolutionary Catechism[1]?

A. The basis of this book was called *The Doctrines of The Salvation Army*, and it enjoyed several editions over the turn of the last century. General William Booth, one of the founders of The Salvation Army, wrote it with the subtitle, "Prepared for the use of Cadets in Training for Officership."

It employed a handy question and answer format, making it easy to access and extract needed information. As the original title suggests, it dealt entirely with doctrinal issues of the day.

This was a street-level apologetic, eminently useful for daily evangelistic conversation.

So, the first half of this book – the part on Salvation Army doctrine, is an updated version of Booth's 1903 book. It is substantively by William Booth, with some arcane language edited and updated, and some supplements and explanatory endnotes added.

But, as soldiers of The Salvation Army know, the Soldier's Covenant, formerly officially known as the Articles of War, includes two sides: the left, addressing orthodoxy (or correct thinking), and the right, dealing with orthopraxy (or correct practice).[2]

And so the second half of the book, addressing the orthopraxy portion (correct practice) with commentary of the former and current declarations of the Articles of War, is written completely by Court.

With the increasing complexity of the Salvation War in the third millennium, some soldiers are looking for some practical, accessible support and direction on both of these issues. Zealous warriors crave the challenge and guidance to optimize effectiveness in the Great Commission warfare.

Q. What's so revolutionary about it?

A. In its DNA, there is nothing conventional about The Salvation Army. It is revolutionary in its birth, ethos, historic goals, and system. And this catechism is revolutionary in both adjective form and noun form.

That is, the book is an adjective, intending to incite a spiritual revolution that overthrows the ruling powers of the prince of the power of the air[3], the god of this age[4] and spiritual forces of evil[5], and frees the global population. Predictable, unadventurous, hesitant lifestyles cannot hope to transform the world.

And it is also a noun, for revolutionaries, those who, with God through The Salvation Army, have plunged into one of history's most hardcore covenants: to engage in worldwide spiritual revolution.

Q. Where does the term *Articles of War* originate?

A. There is some debate about the origins of the term, but the earliest reference we can find is as follows:

> In July 1621, several regiments of the Swedish army were assembled at Arsta Meadow south of Stockholm awaiting transport by ship to the Baltic, where they were to fight the Russian forces which had invaded the provinces in early summer. It was on this occasion that they heard for the first time the new *Articles of War* read to them by chancellor Axel Oxenstierna. The text had been drafted by King Gustavus himself and revised by Oxenstierna the preceding spring, and the final decree had been signed by the King at camp on 15 July.[6]

Kenneth Ogren explains the significance of the original *Articles of War*:

> The *Articles* were indeed new in certain respects, but they were also based on familiar continental models and earlier Swedish texts. They borrowed something from the

> code of Ferdinand of Hungary (1526), something from the famous code of Maximilian II (1570) and something from the code of Maurice of Nassau (1590). The presence of numerous transcripts of continental codes in the Stockholm archives makes it clear that great care was taken to consult the systems used abroad. Yet the *Articles* differed in certain important respects from other codes of military law of that age. Earlier codes were closer in nature to an agreement between contracting parties, whereas King Gustavus' text comprised a set of orders.[7]

The British Royal Navy developed Articles of War in the 1650s to govern the execution of war.[8]

> The Articles of War on board a Royal Navy ship assumed the proportions and gravity of holy writ. It served as the law and *axis mundi* of the secular religion practiced upon His Majesty's Ships otherwise known as the Service. It was read at least once a month, usually when church was rigged on Sunday, and when punishment was inflicted.[9]

Q. How does it come about that The Salvation Army has Articles of War?

A. Midway through history's greatest revival (to that point in time), in 1882, the Articles of War were introduced for new recruits, to focus personal conduct and loyalty in the execution of the Salvation War. By 1890 it was made mandatory that every salvation soldier must, "consider, accept, and then sign this document." Here are the official reasons:

- That they may understand beforehand the doctrines, principles, and practices to which they will have to conform.
- Thinking and praying over these Articles will help him to find out whether he really has the faith and spirit of a salvation soldier or not.
- The pledge involved in signing these articles will help him to be faithful to the Army in the future.
- They prevent many joining who are not in heart and head with us, and who consequently would be likely afterwards to create dissatisfaction and division.[10]

Q. What of this war? What is its purpose?

A. The Salvation Army has a divine mission to win the world for Jesus. Catherine Booth, one of the founders, prophesied:

> The decree has gone forth that the kingdoms of this world shall become the kingdom of our Lord and of His Christ, and that He shall reign, whose right it is, from the River to the ends of the earth. We shall win. It is only a question of time. I believe that this Movement is to inaugurate the great final conquest of our Lord Jesus Christ.[11]

Revolutionary! This significant word was given to mark the initial expansion of The Salvation Army beyond the British Isles on its global Great Commission odyssey.[12] We have been entrusted with a significant role in capturing, for Jesus, those bound by the enemy:

> After this I saw a vast crowd, too great to count, from every nation and tribe and people and language, standing in front of the throne and before the Lamb. They were clothed in white and held palm branches in their hands. And they were shouting with a mighty shout, "Salvation comes from our God on the throne and from the Lamb!"
> *(Revelation 7:9,10 NLT)*

So, every nation, every tribe, every people, and every language will be represented in the great harvest of the last days.[13]

Q. How do we accomplish this mission? How do we fulfill this prophecy?

A. There are two answers. First we must see ourselves as God dreamed up, The Salvation Army being a revolutionary movement of covenanted warriors exercising holy passion to win the world for Jesus. The second elaborates on the "covenanted" part of this identity statement. The grand distinctive of The Salvation Army is our covenant, which is being analyzed and explicated in the following pages.[14] The Articles of War provide the context for covenant community and rein zeal so that as a movement we *can* inaugurate the final conquest.[15]

Q. Why a Reading Club Guide?

A. ARTICLES OF WAR makes it easy for you and your friends or small group or cell or Bible study or Home League to tackle the contents together. Each section has a set of questions that you can discuss when your group meets.

Reading Club Guide

Why use the term "Articles of War"?

How can we position ourselves so that God can fulfill Catherine Booth's prophecy?

What role has covenant played in your life?
(The subject gets more attention later on in the book.)

Is it wrong to be aggressive in our Christianity?

---

[1] A catechism is a summary of the Christian principles in the form of questions and answers, used for the instruction of Christians. It is by Booth and Court because the basis of the first half of the book is Booth's original document which has been edited, updated, and supplemented significantly by Court, and the second half is written by Court. The endnotes are by Court.

[2] The spiritual footnotes of the Soldier's Covenant are the Handbook of Doctrine—Salvation Story for the left side of orthodoxy, and the Orders and Regulations—Chosen To Be A Soldier, for the right side of orthopraxy. Orthopraxy derives from a Greek term and means "correct practice" or right action. There are some versions of the Articles of War that actually place the doctrines on top and the declaration on the bottom. While it doesn't help the illustration, it doesn't hurt the point.

[3] Ephesians 2:1-2.

[4] 2 Corinthians 4:4.

[5] Ephesians 6:12.

[6] Kenneth Ogren. August 8, 1996. "Humanitarian law in the Articles of War decreed in 1621 by King Gustavus II Adolphus of Sweden." in International Review of the Red Cross no 313, p.438-442.

(https://www.icrc.org/eng/resources/documents/article/other/57jn8d.htm)

[8] Gibbons Burke. The Articles of War. 1749.

The 1749 version contained 36 Articles of War, the first two of which we include here. Their Christian content is outstanding to 21st century ears:

1. All commanders, captains, and officers, in or belonging to any of His Majesty's ships or

vessels of war, shall cause the public worship of Almighty God, according to the liturgy of the Church of England established by law, to be solemnly, orderly and reverently performed in their respective ships; and shall take care that prayers and preaching, by the chaplains in holy orders of the respective ships, be performed diligently; and that the Lord's day be observed according to law.

2. All flag officers, and all persons in or belonging to His Majesty's ships or vessels of war, being guilty of profane oaths, cursings, execrations, drunkenness, uncleanness, or other scandalous actions, in derogation of God's honor, and corruption of good manners, shall incur such punishment as a court martial shall think fit to impose, and as the nature and degree of their offence shall deserve.

Q. How else is the term Articles of War used in history?

A. The term is employed since the 1600s for the guidelines and rules governing personal conduct and loyalty in the execution of war. For example, the Continental Congress, in 1775, established Articles of War for the War of Independence against Britain.[9] The US Civil War used it.[9] The United States instituted several versions of the Articles of War between 1912 and 1920.[9] Joseph Goebbels, Nazi Propaganda Minister, presented 30 Articles of War for the German People, in 1943.[9] The Geneva Convention contains Articles of War on the treatment of prisoners of war.[9] The Iraq Conflict during the first decade of this 21st century has drawn on the interpretation and application of Articles of War.[9]

[10] The Salvation Army International Heritage Centre. Articles of War—Origins.

[11] The War Cry (UK). February 21, 1880. p1. The context was her farewell to Alice Coleman, Rachel Evans, Emma Elizabeth Florence Morris, Elizabeth

Pearson, Clara Price, Annie Shaw, and Emma Westbrook (the Hallelujah Lasses) and George Scott Railton deploying to invade America.

[12] Booth is not suggesting that the Army will win the world for Jesus by itself. It sounds like she is indicating the role that the Army is to play—like an arrowhead going in front, making first impact, and opening things up for the rest of the People of God. This interpretation fits the definition that The Salvation Army is the fist of the body of Christ.

[13] See Wesley Campbell and Stephen Court, Be A Hero, 2004, for a historical context, an analysis of the current world scene, and a plan.

[14] The argument of distinctives can be helpful but this is not our purpose here. Instead, we emphasize the Articles of War covenant as being the one thing from a human perspective that can hold The Salvation Army together over the next generation and as an umbrella that contains many of the values that tend to make "distinctives" lists (e.g. holiness, covenant, evangelism, care for the poor, simplicity, etc.).

[15] Those not sold yet on covenant, we want you to hang in there. We will discuss your issues in part 2 of the book. Shared identity blesses diverse ministry. In Revolution in the Church, Michael Brown insists that the readers don't jump ahead. But since you bought this book, we'll let you jump ahead if you feel it absolutely necessary.

PART 1 | Section 1

The Doctrines

What are the doctrines of The Salvation Army?

These are the doctrines of The Salvation Army[1]:

We believe that the Scriptures of the Old and New Testaments were given by inspiration of God, and that they only constitute the Divine rule of Christian faith and practice.

We believe that there is only one God, who is infinitely perfect, the Creator, Preserver, and Governor of all things, and who is the only proper object of religious worship.

We believe that there are three persons in the Godhead-the Father, the Son and the Holy Ghost, undivided in essence and co-equal in power and glory.

We believe that in the person of Jesus Christ the Divine and human natures are united, so that He is truly and properly God and truly and properly man.

We believe that our first parents were created in a state of innocency, but by their disobedience they lost their purity and happiness, and that in consequence of their fall all men have become sinners, totally depraved, and as such are justly exposed to the wrath of God.

We believe that the Lord Jesus Christ has by His suffering and death made an atonement for the whole world so that whosoever will may be saved.

We believe that repentance towards God, faith in our Lord Jesus Christ, and regeneration by the Holy Spirit, are necessary to salvation.

We believe that we are justified by grace through faith in our Lord Jesus Christ and that he that believeth hath the witness in himself.

We believe that continuance in a state of salvation depends upon continued obedient faith in Christ.

We believe that it is the privilege of all believers to be wholly sanctified, and that their whole spirit and soul and body may be preserved blameless unto the coming of our Lord Jesus Christ.

We believe in the immortality of the soul; in the resurrection of the body; in the general judgment at the end of the world; in the eternal happiness of the righteous; and in the endless punishment of the wicked.

---

[1] The following is the doctrines list in 1903. Note that doctrines ix and x are expanded from the current versions, that the final clause of iii appears now at the end of ii, and that "endless" replaces "everlasting" in xi:

i. We believe that the Scriptures of the Old and New Testaments were given by inspiration of God and that they only constitute the Divine rule of Christian faith and practice.

ii. We believe that three is only one God, who is infinitely perfect, the Creator, Preserver, and Governor of all things.

iii. We believe that there are three persons in the Godhead—the Father, the Son, and the Holy Ghost—undivided in essence, co-equal in power and glory, and the only proper object of religious worship.

iv. We believe that in the person of Jesus Christ the Divine and human natures are united, so that He is truly and properly God, and truly and properly man.

v. We believe that our first parents were created in a state of innocency, but by their disobedience they lost their purity and happiness; and that, in consequence of their fall, all men have become sinners, totally depraved, and as such are justly exposed to the wrath of God.

vi. We believe that the Lord Jesus Christ has, by His suffering and death, made an atonement for the whole world, so that whosoever will may be saved.

vii. We believe that repentance toward God, faith in our Lord Jesus Christ, and regeneration by the Holy Spirit, are necessary to salvation.

viii. We believe that we are justified by grace through faith in our Lord Jesus Christ, and that he who believeth hath the witness in himself.

ix. We believe that the Scriptures teach that not only does continuance in the favor of God depend upon continued faith in, and obedience to, Christ, but that it is possible for those who have been truly converted to fall away and be eternally lost.

x. We believe that it is the privilege of all believers to be "wholly sanctified," and that "the whole spirit and soul and body" may be "preserved blameless unto the coming of our Lord Jesus Christ." That is to say, we believe that after conversion there remain in the heart of the believer inclinations to evil or roots of bitterness, which, unless overpowered by Divine grace, produce actual sin; but that these evil tendencies can be entirely taken away by the Spirit of God, and the whole heart, thus cleansed from everything contrary to the will of God, or entirely sanctified, will then produce the fruit of the Spirit only. And we believe that persons thus entirely sanctified may, by the power of God, be kept "unblamable" and "unreprovable" before Him.

xi. We believe in the immortality of the soul; in the resurrection of the body; in the general judgement at the end of the world; in the eternal happiness of the righteous, and in the everlasting punishment of the wicked.

PART 1 | Section 2

God

1. You believe in God. Why?

We believe in the existence of God for four reasons.

2. What is the first?

Look around. We see overwhelming evidence in the world around us. The things that are made shout out that there must be a maker.[1]

For instance, we see a house and are convinced that the house didn't just show up by chance, but that, at some time or another, it must have had a builder. When we see a watch, we are equally sure that there must have been, somewhere, somebody smart enough and skilled enough to make that watch. In the same way, looking at the sun, or the ocean, or a human being, with all the wonderful properties and activities ascribed to each, and we are equally sure that some being who is smart enough, and skilled enough, and powerful enough, equal to the task, must have made that sun, that ocean, that human being. And common sense affirms that the maker of suns and oceans and human beings is the maker of all things that exist, and that this maker of all things must be God.

3. And, secondly?

Our own souls confirm that there must be a God. We've always felt this way, and everybody else feels the same.[2] Only fools say in their hearts, or with their mouths, that there is no God, until, at least, they are on their deathbeds, when the truth usually comes out.

Only fools say in their hearts, "There is no God."
(Psalm 53:1 NLT)

4. What is the third reason?

We believe that there is a God because we have felt Him at work in our own lives, forgiving our sins, changing our hearts, comforting us in sorrow, and making us joyful in Him.[3]

5. And your fourth reason?

The Bible, a true and good book, declares that there is a God, and describes His wonderful works among us.[4]

6. How do you describe God?

God is omnipotent, eternal, independent, self-existent, omniscient, and perfectly wise, good, holy, just, and true.

7. Are there more gods than one?

There is only one true God.

You are my witnesses – is there any other God? No! There is no other Rock – not one! (*Isaiah 44:8 NLT*)

Hear, O Israel! The LORD is our God, the LORD alone. *(Deuteronomy 6:4 NLT)*

8. But you pray to Jesus Christ and to the Holy Spirit as well as to the Father. How is this, if they are not gods?

Although there is only one God, yet, in a mysterious way, the Scripture reveals, there are three persons in the Godhead: the Father, the Son, and the Holy Spirit. Each person in the Godhead is divine, and must be worshipped as God, and they are not three gods, but one God.

9. How is this doctrine described?

This is the Trinity of the Godhead.

10. Do you have any Scriptural support for this doctrine?

Yes, the Bible is full of it.[5] The same words used to declare that Jesus Christ is God and that the Holy Spirit is God are used to confirm that the Father is God.

The same names and titles are given to each, the same amazing works are reportedly performed by each.[6]

And the same worship is offered and commanded to be offered to the Son and the Holy Ghost as is offered and commanded to be offered to the Father.

11. How about a Scripture passage to back this doctrine up?

Yes. The form in which the Apostle Paul sends his blessing to the Corinthian Christians:

> May the grace of our Lord Jesus Christ, the love of God, and the fellowship of the Holy Spirit be with you all. *(2 Corinthians 13:13 NLT)*

12. What is your duty to this benevolent God?

Our duty is consistently, and with all our power, to live, worship, obey, and serve Him, and to do all that we possibly can to persuade everybody else do the same.

Reading Club Guide

Is there a God? How do you know personally?

What is He like? What is His character?

How does your understanding of the Trinity express itself

through your corporate worship and daily life?

How can you improve your relationship with God?

---

[1] "For ever since the world was created, people have seen the earth and sky. Through everything God made, they can clearly see his invisible qualities—his eternal power and divine nature. So they have no excuse for not knowing God" (Romans 1:20 NLT).

[2] "Though many might not admit it. He has planted eternity in the human heart" (Ecclesiastes 3:11 NLT).

[3] "For His Spirit joins with our spirit (or, testifies, in NIV) to affirm that we are God's children" (Romans 8:16 NLT).

[4] It is the only "holy" book that is historically, scientifically, geographically, and prophetically reliable (i.e. what it says touching on these disciplines is true and consistent of findings in those fields).

2 Timothy 3:16 "All Scripture is inspired by God and is useful to teach us what is true and to make us realize what is wrong in our lives. It corrects us when we are wrong and teaches us to do what is right." God breathed it out; He didn't breathe into some existing human text.

There are heaps of available ancient manuscripts: 5,000 Greek manuscripts, 10,000 Latin manuscripts, and 9,000 other languages within 300 years of the original. To set these numbers in perspective, there are only 10 copies of Caesar, 20 copies of Tacitus, and seven copies of Plato, all 1,000 to 1,200 years after the originals.

The Bible is chock full of prophecies, more than 2,000, none of which has failed. Meanwhile, no other holy book even pretends such prescience.

The Bible is even reliable scientifically. No, the Bible is not a science textbook. But it includes in its pages many allusions that can be tested scientifically. And in those cases, it is accurate, often supernaturally so. For example, it consistently spoke truth before the conventional science of even relatively recent history discovered it:

- Every star is different (1 Corinthians 15:41). Science used to believe that that all stars were the same.
- Light is in motion (Job 38:19,20). Science used to believe that light is fixed in place.
- Air has weight (Job 28:25). Science used to believe that air was weightless.
- Wind blows in cyclones (Ecclesiastes 1:6). Science used to believe wind blows straight.

- Blood is the source of life and healing (Leviticus 17:11). Science used to believe that sick people must be bled (source: Hugh Ross, Reasons to Believe, reasons.org).

And, of course, the Bible indicates that the earth is a sphere (Isaiah 40:22), while it took science quite a while to get away from the flat earth belief. The Bible also mentions other scientific fundamentals in passing, such as conversation of mass and energy (Ecclesiastes 1:9; 3:14-15), water cycle (Ecclesiastes 1:7; Isaiah 55:10), gravity (Job 26:7; Job 38:31-33), control of contagious diseases (Leviticus 13:45-46), importance of sanitation to health (Leviticus; Numbers 19; Deuteronomy 23:12-13), effect of emotions on physical health (Proverbs 16:24; 17:22), and that Pleiades and Orion are gravitationally bound star groups Job 38:31 (note: all others, visible to the naked eye, with the possible exception of Hyades, are unbound. source: Hugh Ross, Reasons to Believe, reasons.org). It is safe to conclude that the only points at which science and the Bible differ are those at which science is wrong. So, the Bible is reliable in each and all of these ways.

[5] There is only one God. This is affirmed in many verses, including Deuteronomy 6:4; Mark 12:32; 1 Timothy 2:5; and, James 2:19.

[6] The Old Testament intimates that there are three Persons in the Godhead in verses such as Genesis 1:26 and Isaiah 48:16. In the New Testament the three Persons are mentioned together in such verses as Matthew 3:16,17; Matthew 28:19; 1 Corinthians 12:4-6; and, 2 Corinthians 13:14. Now, God the Father is made clear in verses such as 1 Corinthians 8:6, 2 Corinthians 6:17,18; and, Luke 12:30, 32. Jesus as God is made clear in such verses as Isaiah 9:6; John 1:1; John 20:28; Acts 20:28; Titus 2:13; 2 Peter 1:1; and 1 John 5:20 (see SA Handbook of Doctrine for lists of verses describing aspects of His deity). Holy Spirit as God emerges from such verses as Acts 5:3,4; Isaiah 6:8,9 and Acts 28:25. His eternal existence is evident in Hebrews 9:14. His omnipotence is suggested in Job 33:4. His omnipresence is implied in Psalm 139:7. His omniscience is intimated in 1 Corinthians 2:10. He was involved in the beginning at creation (Genesis 1:2). He regenerates (Titus 3:5). He raises from the dead (Romans 8:11). He imparts miraculous gifts (Romans 15:19; 1 Corinthians 12:6,11). He enlightens in truth (1 Corinthians 2:12,13; John 16:13). These verses and more (consult The SA Handbook of Doctrine) declare Biblical support for the concept of "Trinity" or "Godhead."

PART 1 | Section 3

Jesus Christ is God

1. You say that Jesus Christ is God. How can you prove this?

From the Bible.

2. What is your biblical argument?

He is very clearly called God in the following and other verses:

Mighty God. *(Isaiah 9:6 NLT)*

He is God, who rules over everything and is worthy of eternal praise! *(Romans 9:5 NLT)*

He is the only true God. *(1 John 5:20 NLT)*

Our great God and Savior, Jesus Christ. *(Titus 2:13 NLT)* *(see also verses such as John 1:1; John 20:28; Acts 20:28; 2 Peter 1:1)*

3. What is your second Bible argument?

Those powers and perfections ascribed to Jesus Christ belong only to God.

Watch this:

i. He has "everlasting" existence *(Isaiah 9:6 NLT)*. He was in the beginning with God. *(John 1:2 NLT)*

He is, "One whose origins are from the distant past." *(Micah 5:2 NLT. NKJV has, "from everlasting.")*

ii. He is omnipotent (all-powerful).
He is "Mighty God." *(Isaiah 9:6 NLT)*
He is "the Almighty." *(Revelations 1:8 NLT)*

iii. He is omnipresent (He is present everywhere). For where two or three gather together because they are Mine, I am there among them. *(Matthew 18:20 NLT)*

iv. He is omniscient (He sees and knows everything). But Jesus on His part would not entrust Himself to them, because He knew all people. *(John 2:24 NLT)*

v. He is unchangeable. Jesus Christ is the same yesterday, today, and forever. *(Hebrews 13:8 NLT)*

vi. He possesses every attribute of the Father God. For in Him the whole fullness of deity dwells bodily. *(Colossians 2:9 NRSV)*[1]

4. What is the third biblical argument you bring to prove that Jesus Christ is a Divine Being?

The Bible clearly describes Jesus performing works that only supernatural power could accomplish.

i. The work of creation is said to have been performed by Jesus. He created everything there is. Nothing exists that He didn't make. *(John 1:3 NLT)*

But although the world was made through Him, the world didn't recognize Him when He came. *(John 1:10 NLT)*

Christ is the one through whom God created everything in heaven and earth. He made the things we can see and the things we can't see – kings, kingdoms, rulers, and authorities. Everything has been created through Him and for Him. *(Colossians 1:16 NLT)*

ii. The government of this world is in His hands. I have been given complete authority in heaven and on earth. *(Matthew 28:18 NLT)*

iii. Jesus forgives sins. Take heart, son! Your sins are forgiven. *(Matthew 9:2 NLT)*

Remember, the Lord forgave you, so you must forgive others. *(Colossians 3:13 NLT)*

iv. He will raise the dead and judge the world And the Father leaves all judgment to his Son. *(John 5:22 NLT)*

And He has given Him authority to judge all mankind because He is the Son of Man. *(John 5:27 NLT)*

And He ordered us to preach everywhere and to testify that Jesus is ordained of God to be the judge of all – the living and the dead. *(Acts 10:42 NLT)*

5. What is the fourth argument you produce from Scripture for the Divinity of Jesus Christ?

People worshipped Jesus.[2]

i. People worshipped Jesus. "We have come to worship Him." *(Matthew 2:2 NLT)*

"Then the disciples worshipped him." *(Matthew 14:33 NLT)*

"Yes, Lord," the man said, "I believe!" And he worshipped Jesus. *(John 9:38 NLT)*

"My Lord and my God!" Thomas exclaimed. *(John 20:28 NLT)*

While He was blessing them, He left them and was taken up to heaven. They worshipped Him and then returned to Jerusalem filled with great joy. *(Luke 24:51,52; see also Matthew 28:9,17, etc. NLT)*

"O Lord," they said, "you know every heart. Show us which of these men you have chosen." *(Acts 1:24. NLT)*

And as they stoned him, Stephen prayed, "Lord Jesus, receive my spirit." And he fell to his knees, shouting, "Lord, don't charge them with this sin!" And with that, he died. *(Acts 7:59,60 NLT)*

"And from Jesus Christ, who is the faithful witness to these things, the first to rise from the dead, and the commander of all the rulers of the world. All praise to Him who loves us and has freed us from our sins by shedding His blood for us. He has made us His Kingdom and His priests who serve before God His Father. Give to Him everlasting glory! He rules forever and ever! Amen! *(Revelation 1:5,6 NLT)*

ii. Angels worshipped Jesus. And again, when God brings His firstborn into the world, He says, "Let all the angels of God worship Him." *(Hebrews 1:6 NLT)*

Then I looked again, and I heard the singing of thousands and millions of angels around the throne and the living beings and the elders. And they sang in a mighty chorus:

"The Lamb is worthy- the Lamb who was killed. He is worthy to receive power and riches and wisdom and strength and honor and glory and blessing." *(Revelation 5:11,12 NLT)*

iii. All creatures are to worship Jesus.

Because of this, God raised Him up to the heights of heaven and gave Him a name that is above every other name, so that at the name of Jesus every knee will bow, in heaven and on earth and under the earth, and every tongue will confess that Jesus Christ is Lord, to the glory of God the Father. *(Philippians 2:9-11 NLT)*

6. Do you have a fifth argument from the Bible that supports the divinity of Jesus Christ?

Jesus claimed to be Divine.[3]

All that the Father has is Mine; this is what I mean when I say that the Spirit will reveal to you whatever He receives from Me. *(John 16:15 NLT)*

The Father and I are one. *(John 10:30 NLT)*[4]

7. Do you have any more biblical arguments?

He claimed such love and service from His followers only properly due a Divine Being.

> All those who want to be My disciples must come and follow Me, because My servants must be where I am. And if they follow Me, the Father will honor them.
> *(John 12:26 NLT. See also Matthew 10:27-38)*

8. What's the big argument from those who deny the Divinity of our Lord Jesus?

They like to quote passages that describe or declare His humanity.

9. How do you respond to that?

These texts only prove a truth we hold as strongly as they or anyone else can do. The thing is, as strongly as we believe Jesus to be human, we believe that He is God. He became a human to suffer; He was God so that He could atone.[5]

10. Have you any extra-biblical argument for this essential truth?

Yes. We argue from personal experience of Jesus Christ as Savior, that He has proven in every way worthy of our supreme love and worship and service.

11. What has He done for you that only God could do?

Where to begin? He has pardoned our sins, reconciled us to the Father, delivered us from the power of sin and the Devil, and He keeps and comforts us daily in this mighty conflict. He gives us a holy assurance that He will, if we prove faithful, finally give us a crown of life.

12. Summing it up, then, you are really sold that Jesus Christ is actually God, and, thus, due the submission and worship of every person?

We've thrown everything away for this truth. And we're committed to do everything we can to get everyone we can to join us[6] in honoring and serving Him, and we daily appeal to God for the divine energy to fight courageously for Him until we die, when He'll rush us up to see Him in the glory of His heavenly Kingdom.

Reading Club Guide

How do you deal with the dual nature of Christ?

What does it mean to you that, "Jesus, being in very nature God, did not consider equality with God something to be grasped, but made Himself nothing, taking the very nature of a servant, being made in human likeness?"

How does your relationship with Christ show His divinity? How does it show His humanity?

[1] See also John 14:9; 16:15; Colossians 2:9. His eternal existence is clear in Hebrews 7:26 and Revelation 1:11. His omnipotence is evident in Matthew 28:18 and Philippians 3:21. His omnipresence is suggested in Matthew 18:20 and 28:20. His omniscience is hinted at in Colossians 2:3. His unchangeableness is pointed to in Hebrews 13:8 (see SA Handbook of Doctrine for more).

[2] Jews are monotheistic and only properly worship God. Gentiles came to worship Him as well.

[3] The most famous argument in our era is the "Christian Trilemma" by C.S. Lewis. It goes like this: Jesus claimed to be God. Either it is true or it isn't true. Let's assume it isn't true. Then, there are only two options, either He knows it isn't true or He doesn't know it isn't true. If He knew it isn't true and yet told people He was God then He is a liar. If He didn't know it isn't true and yet told people He is a lunatic. Back it up to the first dilemma, that His claim to be God is either true or not true. We've considered "not true." Well, if the claim is true, then He is Lord. Lewis concludes that Jesus is Lord, liar, or lunatic. You can't get away with revering Him as something less than God (e.g. great teacher, prophet, etc.) when He is either a liar or lunatic. We believe that He is Lord.

[4] "One" is "heis" in Greek. Regardless of whether this meant that He and the Father were physically one or united in agreement, the Jews heard blasphemy (correctly, if Jesus was an imposter) and picked up stones to stone Him.

[5] Insofar as a human forfeited some dominion or relinquished some delegated authority or abdicated some power and Satan filled the vacuum, a human had come to take it back (Satan is called the prince of this world in verses such as John 11:15;12:31;14:30 (NIV) and ruler in 16:11 (NASB). Jesus gives disciples authority—"exousia"—in a few places in the Gospels, such as Luke 9:1; 10:19; 19:17). The role of Jesus in atonement is possible because He is the unblemished, sinless Lamb of God, slain from the foundation of the world (see Revelation 13:8).

[6] This is a portion of one recent formulation of The Salvation Army salute: I'm on my way to heaven and I'm doing everything I can to get everyone I can to join me.

PART 1 | Section 4

How we became sinners.

1. What is this whole "soul" thing? What is a soul?

Throughout the years terms like "soul" and "spirit" have been interchanged so that there is overlap in their meaning today. But how about this? That part of you "separate from and independent of" your body might be called your soul.[1]

2. Will this soul die with the body?

No. The soul is immortal; that is, it can never perish.

And how do you benefit if you gain the whole world but lose your own soul in the process? Is anything worth more than your soul? *(Matthew 16:26 NLT)*

3. You often say, when you are talking, that we are all sinners. How is this? Did God make us sinners?

No. God created Adam and Eve, our first parents, perfectly pure, and pronounced them to be good. He also made every provision for them to continue being good and happy, and if they had continued, the world could even now be full of holy, happy people.

"Oh, that you had listened to my commands! Then you would have had peace flowing like a gentle river and righteousness rolling like waves." *(Isaiah 48:18 NLT)*

4. How then did they fall?

God gave Adam and Eve permission to eat of the fruit of every tree in the garden save one; if they ate of that one they were to pay the penalty of death. But Satan enticed them to eat, and they listened to his lies, fell for them, tasted some forbidden fruit, and thus disobeyed God *(see Genesis 3)*.

5. What were the consequences of this act of disobedience for Adam and Eve?

By that act they lost their purity and the favor of God, were driven from Eden, received the sentence of death in their bodies, came under the power of sin and the Devil, and were exposed to the damnation of Hell *(see Genesis 3 for these and other ramifications)*.

6. Where is God's command on this issue?

"But the LORD God gave him this warning: 'You may freely eat any fruit in the garden except fruit from the tree of the knowledge of good and evil. If you eat of its fruit, you will surely die.'" *(Genesis 2:16,17 NLT)*

7. Adam's sin was terrible, wasn't it?

Yes. There was in it the seed of all other sins.

i. There was the sin of unbelief – they disbelieved God, and believed the devil's lie.

ii. There was the sin of covetousness – God had given them the free use of all the trees except one, and they coveted that.

iii. There was the sin of ingratitude. Though they had received so much from God, they were discontented and ungrateful.

iv. There was the sin of pride. They aspired to be like God, and independent of Him.

v. There was the sin of rebellion against God's authority. Though they had a plain command uttered by the voice of God Himself, they dared to resist Him, and do that which He directly said they should not do.

8. What have been the consequences of Adam's sin for us?

i. We have lost the joys of Paradise.

ii. We have all become depraved – that is, deprived of God's presence and power in our souls, and not only that, but actually wicked in inclination.

iii. This depraved nature leads to willful violation of the law of God.

iv. Consequently, we all come under the curse and condemnation of the divine law, and are therefore exposed to its everlasting penalty.

For all have sinned; all fall short of God's glorious standard. *(Romans 3:23 NLT and see Romans 3:18-31)*

9. Does this affect everyone, that is, are we all sinners, and therefore all guilty before God?

Yes. Sin doesn't manifest in all of us the same way. By that we mean that not everyone swears or blasphemes or gets drunk. However, each of us has a natural inclination to sin, to gratify selfish desires, and an utter disinclination to engage the claims of God and suffering humanity.

10. But how do you connect selfishness to sin?

Because the very essence of sin is selfishness. Selfishness gratifies self, without regard to the glory of God, or the wellbeing of humanity. In this sense, drunkards, thieves, adulterers, and all sorts of sinners, live simply to please themselves. They certainly don't do those things for the glory of God or the benefit of humanity. Sinners sin. Selfish people act selfishly. In one sense, the devil epitomizes selfishness; to gratify his malice and revenge against God, he is trying to hurl Him from His throne and damn the whole race.

11. So, proper spirituality is benevolence?

Yes. We're called and enabled to be benevolent, or loving.[2] It is the being given up to doing good and making others happy. This is the religion of Yahweh – God is love. This was the religion of Jesus Christ.

> You know how full of love and kindness our Lord Jesus Christ was. Though He was very rich, yet for your sakes He became poor, so that by His poverty He could make you rich. *(2 Corinthians 8:9 NLT)*
>
> Dear friends, let us continue to love one another, for love comes from God. Anyone who loves is born of God and knows God. But anyone who does not love does not know God-for God is love. *(1 John 4:7,8 NLT)*

12. Are you saying that only a heart of love, manifest in a life of benevolence, is acceptable to God on earth, and a proper preparation for heaven?

Yes. Love fulfills the law, for love is of God, and everyone that loves is born of God. Even if you donate everything you own to feed the poor, and if your faith enables you to perform miracles, and if your efforts result in many sinners getting saved, and if you get martyred by the flame, and if you possess every other gift given by God to humans, even then, if you aren't moved and filled with love you might as well just be banging on pots and pans.

> If I could speak in any language in heaven or on earth but didn't love others, I would only be making meaningless noise like a loud gong or a clanging cymbal. *(1 Corinthians 13:1 NLT)*

13. But how can such an enormous change happen?

Only the mighty power of the Holy Spirit can pull it off, in the hearts of those who trust our Lord Jesus Christ to make them each a new creation.

14. How can anyone live such a life of love as is required by God without being saved?

You can't; it is useless for people to strive to keep the holy, benevolent law of God with selfish, unholy hearts. They must come to Jesus and be saved.

I assure you, unless you turn from your sins and become as little children, you will never get into the Kingdom of Heaven. *(Matthew 18:3 NLT)*

15. Isn't this where many independents (those who don't yet depend on Jesus) get it wrong?

Yes. They might admire the moral life, and even aim to live up to its standards of benevolence and sacrifice. But they entirely lack power to stem and change the current of their own evil natures. So, they usually give up.

16. What is their only hope?

Jesus Christ. He is the Way, and the only Way, to goodness. He will save them not only from condemnation and perdition, but also from their natural inclination to act selfishly. And He'll send them the Holy Spirit, who will empower them to do right and love God and everything and everybody.

Reading Club Guide

Why is sin a taboo subject these days?

Why is hell often left out of the Gospel story?

Have you properly dealt with your sins?

How have you changed since your sins have been forgiven?

How has Jesus been your only hope?
Can you share your testimony?

---

[1] Some, today, like to explain that we consist of spirit, soul, and body. Spirit is what communicates at a spiritual level. Soul is that which communicates at a human level. And body is the part of you that communicates at a physical level. In the 19th century "soul" is what some understand, in the 21st century, as "spirit."

[2] From Latin—well and willing; goodwill.

PART 1 | Section 5

Redemption

1. What is Redemption?

Redemption is the work of redeeming or delivering from bondage by sacrifice; buying back out of pawn. So Jesus Christ aims to redeem us from the claims of the broken law, and from sin, and Satan, and hell, by the payment of His own blood.

2. What does God aim to accomplish for humanity in the work of redemption?

He aims to restore us from all the effects of the Fall, and to raise us to a position holier, happier, and more secure than that which was forfeited by Adam.[1]

3. How does God aim to accomplish this?

By the life, suffering, and death of our Lord Jesus Christ, and by the Holy Spirit working directly in the world through an army of the redeemed, those who have been washed from their sins in the blood of Jesus Christ and are now spiritual dependents *(dependent on Jesus)*.

4. You have told us that Jesus Christ was God; was He also human?

Yes, He was as truly man as He was truly God. For our sakes He came from Heaven, took upon Himself human nature, and thus made it possible for Him to suffer in our place.[2]

Without question, this is the great mystery of our faith:

> Christ appeared in the flesh and was shown to be righteous by the Spirit. He was seen by angels and was announced to the nations. He was believed on in the world and was taken up into heaven. *(1 Timothy 3:16 NLT Some manuscripts start with "God appeared in the flesh")*

5. What did the Savior do for us?

i. He revealed the Father's will in His teaching.

ii. He left a perfect example for us to imitate.

iii. He atoned for our sins in His death.

6. What is Atonement?

The word means "at-one-ment," and it signifies the way that Jesus Christ opened, in order that God and humans, now separated by sin, may be reunited.

> "For God was in Christ, reconciling the world to Himself, no longer counting people's sins against them. This is the wonderful message He has given us to tell others." *(2 Corinthians 5:19 NLT)*

"Yes, Adam's one sin brought condemnation upon everyone, but Christ's one act of righteousness makes all people right in God's sight and gives them life." *(Romans 5:18 NLT)*

"But now you belong to Christ Jesus. Though you once were far away from God, now you have been brought near to him because of the blood of Christ.

> "For Christ himself has made peace between us Jews and you Gentiles by making us all one people. He has broken down the wall of hostility that used to separate us. By His death He ended the whole system of Jewish law that excluded the Gentiles. His purpose was to make peace between Jews and Gentiles by creating in Himself one new person from the two groups. Together as one body, Christ reconciled both groups to God by means of His death, and our hostility toward each other was put to death." *(Ephesians 2:13-16 NLT)*

7. Can you describe more plainly how we benefit by Jesus' death?

The Father pitied us when He saw us cursed and condemned to everlasting death, and greatly desired to forgive us and make us happy again, but then He had to consider the welfare of others, and the honor of the law we had broken. If He had forgiven us without the sacrifice of His Son, the inhabitants of other worlds and the angels of Heaven might have said: "Oh, it does not matter about breaking His laws; you have only to say you are sorry, and He will make things right." And so God's holy laws would have been disparaged, denigrated, and maligned. To solve this problem, Jesus Christ, the Father's only Son, came and suffered as a sacrifice for us, and so magnified the importance of the law we had broken, while, at the same time, making a way for our deliverance from its penalty.

8. Is not Jesus' death sometimes described as a "satisfaction" to divine justice?

Yes. Jesus' death satisfied divine justice, inasmuch as –

i. Our sins deserved death.

ii. Christ voluntarily died in our place.

iii. In virtue of His dignity as God, and His purity as Man, His sacrifice possessed of infinite merit, and fully met the claims of the law, and justified God in remitting the punishment, and in forgiving all who repent and believe on Him.

9. Do you have any Scripture to back you up on this doctrine?

i. There are texts in which Christ is a ransom for mankind. The word "ransom" signifies the price paid for the deliverance of a captive *(e.g. Matthew 20:28)*. The word "ransom" in 1 Timothy 2:6 – "Who gave himself a ransom for all" – signifies the ransom paid for the life of a captive, by giving up the life of another person, the idea, in both cases being that of "substitution" or "satisfaction."

ii. Those passages which speak of Christ as being the Redeemer of the race—

For you know that God paid a ransom to save you from the empty life you inherited from your ancestors. And the ransom He paid was not mere gold or silver. He paid for you with the precious lifeblood of Christ, the sinless, spotless Lamb of God. *(1 Peter 1:18,19 NLT)*

For God bought you with a high price. So you must honor God with your body. *(1 Corinthians 6:20 NLT)*

He is so rich in kindness that He purchased our freedom through the blood of His Son, and our sins are forgiven. *(Ephesians 1:7 NLT)*

And now beware! Be sure that you feed and shepherd God's flock-his church, purchased with His blood—over whom the Holy Spirit has appointed you as elders. *(Acts 20:28 NLT)*

And since we have been made right in God's sight by the blood of Christ, He will certainly save us from God's judgment. *(Revelation 5:9 NLT)*

iii. Those passages which speak of Christ as being the substitute for sinners—

But God showed his great love for us by sending Christ to die for us while we were still sinners. *(Romans 5:8 NLT)*

I passed on to you what was most important and what had also been passed on to me—that Christ died for our sins, just as the Scriptures said. *(1 Corinthians 15:3 NLT)*

Whatever we do, it is because Christ's love controls us. Since we believe that Christ died for everyone, we also believe that we have all died to the old life we used to live. He died for everyone so that those who receive his new life will no longer live to please themselves. Instead, they will live to please Christ, who died and was raised for them. *(2 Corinthians 5:14,15 NLT)*

He died for our sins, just as God our Father planned, in order to rescue us from this evil world in which we live. *(Galatians 1:4 NLT)*

What we do see is Jesus, who, "for a little while was made lower than the angels," and now is, "crowned with glory and honor," because He suffered death for us. Yes, by God's grace, Jesus tasted death for everyone in all the world. *(Hebrews 2:9 NLT)*

"Christ also suffered when He died for our sins once for all time. He never sinned, but He died for sinners that He might bring us safely home to God. He suffered physical death, but He was raised to life in the Spirit." *(1 Peter 3:18 NLT)*

iv. Those passages which speak of Jesus Christ as making reconciliation, by His death, between us and God—

All this newness of life is from God, who brought us back to himself through what Christ did. And God has given us the task of reconciling people to Him. For God was in Christ, reconciling the world to Himself, no longer counting people's sins against them. This is the wonderful message He Has given us to tell others. *(2 Corinthians 5:18,19 NLT)*

For since we were restored to friendship with God by the death of His Son while we were still His enemies, we will certainly be delivered from eternal punishment by His life. So now we can rejoice in our wonderful new relationship with God—all because of what our Lord Jesus Christ has done for us in making us friends of God. *(Romans 5:10,11 NLT)*

10. Did Jesus Himself teach that He came to atone for all humanity?

Yes. He declared the substitutionary character of His work when He compared himself to the snake lifted up at which the Israelites looked and were delivered—

And as Moses lifted up the bronze snake on a pole in the wilderness, so I, the Son of Man, must be lifted up on a pole, so that everyone who believes in me will have eternal life. *(John 3:14,15 NLT)*

i. When He declared that He gave His life a ransom for many—

   For even I, the Son of Man, came here not to be served but to serve others, and to give my life as a ransom for many. *(Matthew 20:28 NLT)*

ii. When He invites the crowds to eat His flesh and drink His blood, which He will give for the life of the world—

   I am the living bread that came down out of heaven. Anyone who eats this bread will live forever; this bread is My flesh, offered so the world may live… I assure you, unless you eat the flesh of the Son of Man and drink His blood, you cannot have eternal life within you. But those who eat My flesh and drink My blood have eternal life, and I will raise them at the last day …. *(John 6:51-55 NLT)*

iii. When He declares that He is the Good Shepherd, who giveth His life for the sheep—

I am the good shepherd. The good shepherd lays down His life for the sheep. *(John 10:11 NLT)*

iv. When He affirmed that His blood was shed for many for the remission of their sins—

For this is My blood, which seals the covenant between God and His people. It is poured out to forgive the sins of many. *(Matthew 26:28 NLT)*

11. Don't all the prophecies describing the coming Messiah as a Sacrifice for sins find their fulfillment in Jesus?

Yes. For example, Isaiah 53 makes little sense outside of a description of Jesus as sacrifice—

But He was wounded and crushed for our sins. He was beaten that we might have peace. He was whipped, and we were healed! *(Isaiah 53:5,6 NLT)*

Reading Club Guide

Redemption, substitution, satisfaction, reconciliation – which perspective of Jesus' efforts on your behalf is most meaningful to you? Why?

Which aspect of Jesus' redemption is most misunderstood? Why?

How do you react to accounts of Jesus' sacrifice for you?

How has Jesus "made peace" in your life?

---

[1] There is a legitimate question as to how Booth might suggest this position is to be higher, happier, and more secure than that forfeited by Adam. The solution might be that we know forgiveness and all that Jesus' sacrifice that made forgiveness possible entails.

[2] Jesus' humanity gave Him a proper position to engage the enemy (Jesus replaces Adam in a few different ways, for example, 1 Corinthians 15:45). In Matthew 8:28-29, demons recognize Jesus' divinity— "Son of God. Have you come here to torment us before the time?" In Mark 5:6-7, demons fall before Jesus and cry out, "Son of the Most high God… I implore You by God, do not torment me."

Here a demon is calling on God to spare him from Jesus! And he is commanding Jesus to back off. How strange is that? The reason is this: They knew that they'd taken power over the earth over the tragic incident in the Garden (Genesis 3. And their ruler was prince of this world and ruler of this world - John 11:15; 12:31; 14:30 (NIV) and ruler in 16:11 (NASB)). They knew the divine Jesus was coming inevitably, but figured He was too soon, and didn't have the right to interfere. That's why they called on God to step in.

What they didn't know is that Jesus was totally human. That is why He had the right to intervene. Insofar as a human forfeited some dominion or relinquished some delegated authority or abdicated some power and Satan filled the vacuum, a Human had come to take it back (we learned some of this from James Garlow, The Covenant. Garlow was pastor of Skyline Wesleyan Church).

PART 1 | Section 6

The Extent of the Atonement

1. Can the benefits of Christ's atonement extend to all people?

Yes. These benefits were obtained, and are intended for the whole world; that is, for all who have lived in the past, for all who live now, and for all who will follow in the future.

2. How do you prove that Christ died for all people?

i. From what we know of the benevolent character of God we should expect that He would include the whole race in the merciful undertaking. It would appear to us absolute cruelty to leave any out.

ii. There is not a passage in the Bible that says He did not die for all people.

iii. There are many passages in the Bible that say He did die for everyone.

He gave His life to purchase freedom for everyone. This is the message that God gave to the world at the proper time. *(1 Timothy 2:6 NLT)*

We work hard and suffer much in order that people will believe the truth, for our hope is in the living God, who is the Savior of all people, and particularly of those who believe. *(1 Timothy 4:10 NLT)*

What we do see is Jesus, who, "for a little while was made lower than the angels," and now is, "crowned with glory and honor," because He suffered death for us. Yes, by God's grace, Jesus tasted death for everyone in all the world. *(Hebrews 2:9 NLT)*

iv. The Bible also says that Christ died for "the world," the "whole world."

For God so loved the world that He gave His only Son, so that everyone who believes in Him will not perish but have eternal life. *(John 3:16 NLT)*

The next day John saw Jesus coming toward him and said, "Look! There is the Lamb of God who takes away the sin of the world!" *(John 1:29 NLT)*

He is indeed the Savior of the world. *(John 4:42b NLT)*

I am the living bread that came down out of heaven. Anyone who eats this bread will live forever; this bread is My flesh, offered so the world may live. *(John 6:51 NLT)*

3. How does the Calvinist tradition try to explain away these passages?

By saying that it is the "elect world" that is intended here; that is, only every elect person. The problem is that there is no such phrase as the elect world in the whole Bible, so you can't go limiting God's mercy and grace with such fanciful inventions.

4. Do you have any other biblical argument to demonstrate that Jesus died for all?

Most people agree that Christ died for those who are saved, but the Bible positively states that He died for those who will be lost, and so He must have died for everyone.

> And if another Christian is distressed by what you eat, you are not acting in love if you eat it. Don't let your eating ruin someone for whom Christ died. *(Romans 14:15; 1 Corinthians 8:11 NLT)*

> But there were also false prophets in Israel, just as there will be false teachers among you. They will cleverly teach their destructive heresies about God and even turn against their Master who bought them. Theirs will be a swift and terrible end. *(2 Peter 2:1 NLT)*

5. Have you any other argument?

Yes. If Christ did not die for all, how could we urge all sinners to believe He died for them? Unless He died for everyone, you couldn't be sure He died for you, neither could you be condemned, nor condemn yourself for not believing that of which you had no assurance. But Christ did die for everyone, and each person must believe it on the peril of everlasting damnation.

6. Is there any other argument?

The Bible says we are to offer mercy to everyone; but how can we do that, and offer everyone salvation if Christ only died for a portion of the human race?

And then He told them, "Go into all the world and preach the Good News to everyone, everywhere." *(Mark 16:15 NLT)*

Then Jesus said, "Come to Me, all of you who are weary and carry heavy burdens, and I will give you rest." *(Matthew 11:28 NLT)*

On the last day, the climax of the festival, Jesus stood and shouted to the crowds, "If you are thirsty, come to Me!" *(John 7:37 NLT)*

The Spirit and the bride say, "Come." Let each one who hears them say, "Come." Let the thirsty ones come—anyone who wants to. Let them come and drink the water of life without charge. *(Revelation 22:17 NLT)*

Reading Club Guide

Before reading this chapter, what was your view on this subject?

How is this chapter important for daily Christian warfare?

How do you go to Jesus to drink?

What is the significance of believing that Jesus died for "the whole world"?

How does it change the way we live out our faith?

PART 1 | Section 7

The Finished Work of Christ

1. You will sometimes hear people talk about the finished work of Christ. What do they mean?

That Jesus Christ, when He died on the cross, put Himself in the place of the sinner and bore the exact amount of punishment deserved, thus actually paying the debt that the sinner owed to divine justice. And that if the sinner will only believe this, he is forever free from the claims of the law, and can never be brought into condemnation either here or hereafter.

2. Is this true?

No.

3. Why do you think it is not true?

If it were so, if Jesus Christ did literally pay the sinner's debt, in this sense, God cannot justly demand payment twice and consequently no one will be sent to Hell, and all will be saved.[1]

4. But don't those who believe that Jesus Christ did actually and literally pay all the sinner's debt upon the cross also teach that only those who believe it benefit from the payment?

Yes. But if a debt is paid, it is paid, and the sinner's unbelief does not in any way affect the fact. If I owe you $5, and my writing partner pays you back for me, you can't sue me for the sum. I am all right, seeing the debt is paid, whether I believe it or not.

5. But don't they reply that sinners are lost not because they are sinners, seeing that their sins have been borne by Christ, but because they don't believe the fact, and they quote: "Anyone who believes and is baptized will be saved. But anyone who refuses to believe will be con demned" *(Mark 16:16 NLT)***?**

Yes. But anyone can see that if all the sinner's debt has been paid, all the sins of unbelief must have been paid also, otherwise how can his past unbelief be forgiven, and if all his unbelief has been atoned or paid for, how can anyone be sent to hell for that, any more than any other sin?

6. How can anyone consistently hold this doctrine of the literal payment of the sinner's debt?

Only by rejecting the glorious truth that Jesus Christ died for everyone. Those who hold to a limited atonement are at least consistent, because they say that Christ paid the debt of a certain number, and therefore their salvation is secure whatever they do, as Christ cannot die in vain.

7. But isn't this view of the literal payment of debt inconsistent in those who believe that Christ died for everyone?

Yes, indeed. According to this argument, if Christ paid everyone's debt, then everyone will be saved, and so the doctrine leads us to universal salvation.

8. But isn't it true that Jesus Christ did pay our debt when He died for us?

Not in the sense that debts are paid here. Otherwise, as we have seen, those for whom Christ died are forever free, regardless of how they choose to live, because payment cannot be twice demanded.

9. But what is the correct view of the Atonement?

We have already explained it in Section 4.[2] The Scriptures teach that Jesus Christ on the cross, in virtue of the dignity of His person, the voluntary nature of His offering, and the greatness of His sufferings, made, on behalf of poor sinners, a sacrifice of infinite value. And that this sacrifice, by showing all worlds the terrible evil of the sin we had committed and the importance of the law we had broken, made it possible for the love and pity of God to flow out to us by forgiving all those who repent and return in confidence to Him, enabling

Him to be just and yet the justifier of everyone who believes in Jesus.

10. So did Jesus Christ endure the exact amount of suffering that sinners ought to have endured?

We do not know what our blessed Savior suffered, and we never shall, but we do know that His sacrifice is far more likely to make the inhabitants of the universe have a profound respect for the law and justice of God than would have been effected by sending the whole race to hell.

11. Can any one do or suffer anything, either before or after conversion, to MERIT SALVATION in any way?

No. From beginning to end it is all about the love of God manifest in the death and resurrection of Jesus Christ.[3]

Reading Club Guide

What was your perspective on this issue before reading the chapter?

How has it changed?

Why is this issue important?

[1] It may be asserted that verses such as Colossians 2:13,14 suggest differently: "You were dead because of your sins and because your sinful nature was not yet cut away. Then God made you alive with Christ. He forgave all our sins. He cancelled the record that contained the charges against us. He took it and destroyed it by nailing it to Christ's cross." However, Paul and Timothy are talking to Colossian and Laodicean Christians in this text. Even from the perspective that all sins were paid for at the cross, the forgiveness comes in response to repentance and faith (see Acts 2:38; 26:17,18; etc.).

[2] And in the footnotes to section 4.

[3] The context of this comment is the explanation of the doctrine of Salvation, to follow. In a nutshell, Jesus invites/commands, "repent and believe."

PART 1 | Section 8

Election

1. Can you explain what the Calvinist tradition teaches on the doctrine of Election?

Yes. Calvinists teach that God has, out of His mere good pleasure, and for His own glory, from all eternity elected or chosen, without any regard to the faith or conduct of the individuals themselves, a portion of the human race to be saved, and covenanted to bring them to Heaven.

2. But what do they teach God's action to be with regard to those who are not elected?

Calvinists teach that God has from all eternity, of His own good pleasure, and without any regard to their conduct, reprobated or left the remainder of mankind to everlasting damnation.

3. Why are these views called Calvinistic?

Because they were taught with considerable earnestness and ability by the 16th century Swiss Reformer John Calvin and/or his followers.

4. When were these "Calvinistic" doctrines first taught in the church?

They are not found in the writings of any Christian teachers until nearly 300 years after Christ.

5. Some of the favorite Bible passages in the Calvinist tradition appear to teach this doctrine. What do you think?

There are some passages in the Scriptures that seem to lean toward these views, but it is only because they have not been properly translated, or because they are not rightly understood. No passage or passages can be supposed to have a meaning opposed to the general signification of the entire book, and the Bible, taken as a whole, is most emphatically against the doctrines of Calvinism.[1]

6. What are some of these favorite Calvinistic passages apparently supporting these views?

> God the Father chose you long ago, and the Spirit has made you holy. As a result, you have obeyed Jesus Christ and are cleansed by his blood. May you have more and more of God's special favor and wonderful peace. *(1 Peter 1:2 NLT)*

But this does not mean that individuals are elected while in an unconverted state in order to be sanctified, but that through, and on account of the sanctification of the Spirit, they are made of the elect: that is, accepted of God. But their final acceptance still depends on their final perseverance. This election is, therefore, strictly conditional, and although it takes place according to the foreknowledge of God, it is an act of God done in time, and is intended to result in constant obedience, and in the continued realization of the sprinkling of the blood of Christ. This election is therefore conditional. Indeed, there is no other.

7. Give another passage quoted to sustain these views.

> As for us, we always thank God for you, dear brothers and sisters loved by the Lord. We are thankful that God chose you to be among the first to experience salvation, a salvation that came through the Spirit who makes you holy and by your belief in the truth. He called you to salvation when we told you the Good News; now you can share in the glory of our Lord Jesus Christ. *(2 Thessalonians 2:13,14 NLT)*

It is argued that by the term "from the beginning" (in AV; here rendered "among the first") the Apostle here intended to signify that these Thessalonian Christians had been chosen or elected to salvation before the foundation of the world, whereas he simply referred to the fact that they believed, and were, in consequence, saved and chosen to enjoy salvation at "the beginning" of commencement of the preaching of the Gospel in those parts.[2]

8. What other passage do they quote to back it up?

The closing sentence of the parable, "For many are called, but few are chosen" *(Matthew 22:14 NLT)*. This text is supposed to teach that, while the call of salvation is sounded out to many, only a few are elected to comply with it.

9. Is this what the parable means?

No. It is just the opposite. The parable tells of a number of people invited to a wedding banquet feast, a well-known condition of being admitted to which was the wearing of a certain outfit. One man not only refused to put on this garment, but insulted the King by appearing at the feast without it, and was, therefore, very properly tossed out. He was called to the banquet, but the condition of his participating was the wearing of this particular kind of robe. He refused to comply with the condition, and was, accordingly, not chosen to participate in the banquet.

In the same way salvation goes forth to the masses, but only a few comply with the conditions, which are repentance towards God, and obedient faith in our Lord Jesus Christ, and are, therefore, not chosen to enjoy and possess the blessings God has provided for His people.

10. Do they quote any other Election verses?

> When the Gentiles heard this, they were very glad and thanked the Lord for His message; and all who were appointed to eternal life became believers. *(Acts 13:48 NLT)*

This passage, as it stands, certainly suggests that some in the assembly were ordained or chosen to be eternally saved. But, properly translated, it does not mean this. Philip Doddridge, a Calvinist, and a great authority as a Greek scholar, translates the passage thus: "As many as were DETERMINED for eternal life, believed." That is just what we teach. If a man desires, or is determined, to give up sin and believe Jesus Christ, he will be elected, or selected, to be saved. The Greek word appears seven times in the New Testament and is translated "appointed," "designated," "determined," "devoted," "established," and "set" in the New American Standard Bible. The renderings become, "those devoted to eternal life," "those established on eternal life," and "those set on eternal life."

11. Does the Calvinist tradition use Romans chapter 9 to teach this doctrine?

Yes. But, rightly understood, it does not support it. The Election set forth in this chapter consists in the selection by God of Jacob and His Seed to possess and enjoy religious and national privileges, and has no reference whatever to unconditional personal election to everlasting life.

12. How is verse 11 to be understood?

> But before they were born, before they had done anything good or bad, they received a message from God (This message proves that God chooses according to His own plan). *(Romans 9:11 NLT)*

That God's purpose or choice of making a great nation of Jacob should be carried out, and nothing more.

13. How should verse 13 be understood?

> In the words of the Scriptures, "I loved Jacob, but I rejected Esau." *(Romans 9:13 NLT)*

That God regarded Esau and his seed with less favor than Jacob, so far as their national position was concerned, which is a very different thing to reprobating him to everlasting damnation before he was born or had the opportunity of knowing good from evil.

14. How do you explain verse 15?

> For God said to Moses, "I will show mercy to anyone I choose, and I will show compassion to anyone I choose." *(Romans 9:15 NLT)*

This passage, and, indeed, most of the chapter, is an argument aimed at the selfishness and bigotry of the Jews, who were opposed to the Gentiles being brought by the Gospel on to the same platform of privilege and communion as themselves; and the Apostle here argues that as God had, if He saw fit, the right to choose Jacob for this high privilege, and to reject Esau, so now He had the right to reject the Jews on the ground of their unfaithfulness, and to put the Gentiles in their place. All that follows is in the same spirit.

> So you see, God shows mercy to some just because He wants to, and He chooses to make some people refuse to

> listen. *(Romans 9:18 NLT)*

Paul sums up his argument in chapter 9 here:

> Well then, what shall we say about these things? Just this: The Gentiles have been made right with God by faith, even though they were not seeking him. But the Jews, who tried so hard to get right with God by keeping the law, never succeeded. Why not? Because they were trying to get right with God by keeping the law and being good instead of by depending on faith. They stumbled over the great rock in their path. *(Romans 9:30-32 NLT)*

15. What do you understand by the term, "Foreknowledge of God"?

By "foreknowledge" we understand that God foresees, or knows beforehand, what is going to happen.

16. What is the meaning of "predestination"?

By "predestination" people of the Calvinist tradition mean that God has ordered and arranged everything that shall happen or come to pass in the future.

17. What is the difference between predestination and foreknowledge?

To foreknow is simply to see beforehand that certain things

will happen, but to predestinate certain events is to make them happen with absolute certainty.

18. Isn't it frequently taught that God's foreknowledge of events proves that those events are pre-arranged and made to come to pass by Him?

Yes, but this is not the case. The foreknowledge of an event by God does not any more make Him the author of that event than the "after-knowledge" of the event would make me the author of it. Astronomers can foresee—that is, foreknow—an eclipse of the sun, and describe, with the greatest minuteness, the hour and circumstances when it will come to pass, but this, you have to admit, has nothing to do with predestinating or causing the eclipse itself. In the same way, God's foreknowledge of a man's acceptance or rejection of salvation has nothing to do with His acting either one way or the other.

19. How do you explain Romans 8:29?

> For God knew His people in advance, and He chose them to become like His Son, so that His Son would be the firstborn, with many brothers and sisters. *(Romans 8:29 NLT)*

By reading the verse that goes before it.

> And we know that God causes everything to work together for the good of those who love God and are called according to his purpose for them. *(Romans 8:28 NLT)*

And by reading the verses that follow it. They explain that God foresaw who would love Him, receive His Son and salvation, and those people He chose (sometimes rendered "predestinated") to be made like Jesus; and those who obey this choice or call of God, and persevere in conformity to His Son, them He certainly justifies and glorifies.

20. But doesn't this passage prove that every individual person thus predestinated and called will be glorified—that is, finally saved?

Calvinists say it means this, but it does not say so, and any number of other passages in the Bible flatly contradict such an interpretation.[3] Indeed this, as every other promise of final salvation, is made conditional on continued faith and obedience. *(See section 20.)*

21. Why do people misunderstand these and similar texts?

These and similar passages are made to refer to individuals, rather than, as intended, to character. God is no respecter of persons, but He is a respecter of character.

The election of the Bible simply signifies the selection of persons possessing a certain character to enjoy particular blessing or inherit a particular destiny, for which their characters have fitted and prepared them. For instance:

God has, from all eternity, predestinated or predetermined—

- That sinners repenting of sin shall obtain mercy.
- That believers in Jesus Christ shall be saved.
- That rejecters of Jesus Christ shall perish.
- That the saints shall enjoy His favor.
- That those who endure to the end shall be saved.

22. Couldn't God prevent sin?

Not if He still wanted us to have free will. The free will allows us to choose to love Him. It is an essential component of being made in His image. Of course, this free will also means that we can choose to sin.

23. But if God foresaw that Adam would fall and thereby bring all this sin and misery into the world, why did He create him? Or having done so, why did He not destroy him immediately after his transgression?

It comes back to the reality that the best of all possible worlds includes free will—free will that can choose to love God or to sin terribly. This best world, God foresaw, would result despite Adam's sin. If it had been otherwise, then God, as a benevolent Being, would have been obliged to destroy him.

24. This subject is a great mystery, isn't it?

Yes. It has puzzled the most profound minds from the beginning, and many have got out of their depth and lost their way through it. Our wisest course is to leave these speculations and optimize our response to what God has revealed. We know He hates sin, and we believe that He is doing His utmost to get people saved from committing it; and we know also that He fails because He has such a wretched, cowardly set of Soldiers to fight for Him. With true Soldiers, and plenty of them, we have every reason to conclude that He would soon drive sin and the devil out of the world. Let us help Him.

25. What are your main objections to the absolute and unconditional salvation and damnation of people?

First, this teaching is opposed to what we know of the love of God. How could it be said that God loves the world, or that God is love at all, if He sends people to suffer in hell forever, without the possibility of being saved?

26. What other argument do you have against these doctrines?

They are opposed to our sense of justice. That God should practice such manifest favoritism as to select a portion of the human race to go to Heaven, and leave the remainder to go to hell without any regard to their conduct or character, directly and most emphatically contradicts our notions of right and wrong. It is contrary to the plainest teaching of our reason.

27. But isn't it said sometimes that we are to be guided in spiritual things by revelation, and not by reason?

Yes, and so we are, but there is a world of difference between a thing being *above* my reason, and *contrary* to it. We believe many things revealed that are above our reason, but we don't buy that which is contrary to it. And since these doctrines are *not* in the Bible, and are *contrary* to our reason, we reject them.

28. Any other objections to these doctrines?

Not only are they notably absent from the Bible, their arguments are distinctly opposed by the whole tenor of Scripture.

29. For example?

The parable of the Sower *(Matthew 13:3-8, 18-23)*.

In this parable the reason why people are not saved is so clearly stated that even fools should be able to understand it. It is not an absolute and dreadful decree that has left the poor soul outside the circle of loving effort. In fact, the same Sower sows the same seed for the unfruitful and the fruitful. You cannot blame the Sower or the seed. It all comes down to the hearts of those who either accept it or reject it.

30. What other Bible arguments do you have against these doctrines?

All those passages which declare that God wants everyone to be saved, and wants none to be damned. The doctrine of Election, as taught in those decrees, makes Him to be a liar.

> Do you think, asks the Sovereign LORD, that I like to see wicked people die? Of course not! I only want them to turn from their wicked ways and live. *(Ezekiel 18:23 NLT)*

> As surely as I live, says the Sovereign LORD, I take no pleasure in the death of wicked people. I only want them to turn from their wicked ways so they can live. Turn! Turn from your wickedness, O people of Israel! Why should you die? *(Ezekiel 33:11 NLT)*

> The Lord isn't really being slow about His promise to return, as some people think. No, He is being patient for your sake. He does not want anyone to perish, so He is giving more time for everyone to repent. *(2 Peter 3:9 NLT)*

31. Have you any other passages?

Half the Bible. But especially those passages that represent the yearning pity of God for perishing people. Here are two:

> O Jerusalem, Jerusalem, you who kill the prophets and stone those sent to you, how often I have longed to gather your children together, as a hen gathers her chicks under her wings, but you were not willing! *(Luke 8:34 NLT)*

> But as they came closer to Jerusalem and Jesus saw the city ahead, He began to cry. "I wish that even today you would find the way of peace. But now it is too late, and peace is hidden from you." *(Luke 19:41,42 NLT)*

a. Any other Scriptural arguments?

All those passages which teach that Christ died for all.
(See Section 5)

b. Is that all?

No. What an utterly deadly effect they must have upon all concerned, self-sacrificing effort for the salvation of souls! How can you run or fight to snatch people as brands from the burning when you believe they are appointed to perish from eternity? If you know that they are already either elected or not elected, your efforts are useless and entirely unnecessary. They are needless to those people who are elected, for they will infallibly be saved without them; they are useless to those people who are not elected, for with or without them, they will infallibly be damned. Therefore, those who hold these doctrines cannot, consistently with their principles, take any great bother about their salvation.

Reading Club Guide

What was your position on election coming in to this chapter?

How has it changed?

How does this affect your evangelism and discipling of people?

How do you think your response to God would have been different if you believed in predestination?

What is the fruit of repentance in your own life? Discuss.

---

[1] We'll address a few of these in points 6-14.

[2] This is an example of "bad" translation leading to "bad" doctrine. General Booth tackled this verse misused by Calvinists. But the more recent translation makes the meaning clear and thus makes the verse useless to the Calvinist position. Here is the Authorized Version: "But we are bound to give thanks alway to God for you, brethren beloved of the Lord, because God hath from the beginning chosen you to salvation through sanctification of the Spirit and belief of the truth."

[3] Salvation is available to everyone, as is clear from verses such as Acts 4:12; Romans 1:16,17; Mark 16:16; John 3:17; and Romans 10:9-13. Salvation is conditional to those who repent and believe (Mark 1:15,17; Acts 3:19; Luke 13:3; Matthew 4:17; Acts 17:30; Acts 26:20; Ephesians 2:8; Acts 16:30; Hebrews 10:39; etc.). Salvation promises are valid for those who continue to fulfill the conditions (e.g. Matthews 10:22; 24:13; Mark 13:13; etc.).

PART 1 | Section 9

The Holy Spirit

1. What else did Jesus' death do for us?

He obtained for us the presence and operation of the Holy Spirit *(see John 17:7 and following)*.

2. Was the Holy Spirit in the world before Jesus?

Yes, certainly.[1]

3. How do these two answers add up?

The benefits of Christ's death in the work of the Spirit, and otherwise, were anticipated by God, flowing backwards to Abel, or Adam himself, who were as much saved through the blood of Christ as any sinner of our day.

4. But wasn't the Holy Spirit given to the Apostles on the Day of Pentecost?

Yes, the Holy Spirit was given to them, in a special measure then, and, through them, to the world generally. The Day of Pentecost was to the Apostles and early disciples what many all-nights, or special meetings, are to The Salvation Army people nowadays — a day of special endowment for the warfare before them.[2] But the Holy Spirit had been working on humanity from the beginning.

5. How is the Holy Spirit's work essential?

Because people are not only condemned sinners, exposed to the fires of God's wrath, but hardened rebels, in love with their sins, and hating God and all His ways. Rather than wanting to be restored to God and made like Him, there is nothing they are so dead against. Therefore, the Holy Spirit comes to overcome this opposition and induce people to submit to God and be saved.

6. How does the Holy Spirit aim at the submission and salvation of all people?

Jesus sent the Holy Spirit to the disciples. And through them He would, "convince the world of its sin, and of God's righteousness, and of the coming judgment" *(John 16:7,8 NLT)*. The Holy Spirit is filling disciples and deploying them in the fight for God, qualifying them with wisdom, love, and zeal, giving them thoughts and messages direct from Himself, and sustaining and comforting them in the conflict.

7. But doesn't the Holy Spirit speak directly to people's hearts?

Yes, the Holy Spirit speaks directly to the hearts of sinners, persuading and urging them to submit to God and be saved. We know it as prevenient grace. In the same way that Spirit also moves directly upon the hearts of Saints, persuading, guiding, and influencing them in all that concerns their holiness, usefulness, and happiness.

> And when He comes, He will convince the world of its sin, and of God's righteousness, and of the coming judgment. *(John 16:8 NLT)*

> And my message and my preaching were very plain. I did not use wise and persuasive speeches, but the Holy Spirit was powerful among you. I did this so that you might trust the power of God rather than human wisdom.
> *(1 Corinthians 2:4,5 NLT)*

> But when you are arrested and stand trial, don't worry about what to say in your defense. Just say what God tells you to. Then it is not you who will be speaking, but the Holy Spirit. *(Mark 13:11 NLT; see also Luke 12:11; 21:14,15; etc.)*

8. What do you mean by the Spirit speaking DIRECTLY to people's hearts?

We mean that He does not confine Himself to sending messages to people through us, or through books, but He, Himself, goes straight to people's hearts and influences them so as to make them feel what He wants them to do.

9. Can the Spirit of God be resisted?

Yes, unquestionably. People can and do resist the Spirit; that is, they refuse to do what He wants them to do. Sinners refuse to give up their wicked course of conduct, submit to God, and accept mercy.

> You stubborn people! You are heathen at heart and deaf to the truth. Must you forever resist the Holy Spirit? But your ancestors did, and so do you! *(Acts 7:51)*

10. What are the consequences of persisting in this resistance of the Holy Spirit?

Destruction. Long resisted, the Holy Spirit gives sinners up to the badness of their hearts, and leaves them to perish.

> Leave her alone because she is married to idolatry. *(Hosea 4:17 NLT)*

> But they rebelled against Him and grieved His Holy Spirit. That is why He became their enemy and fought against them. *(Isaiah 63:10 NLT)*

> So in my anger I made a vow: "They will never enter My place of rest." *(Psalm 95:11 NLT)*

11. But why do people resist the Holy Spirit like that?

It is because they love their sins, and He offers them no mercy, no comfort, no Savior, no Heaven, on any other condition than GIVING THEM UP. Therefore, they shut up their hearts against Him, and hate Him.

12. Then this shows the real reason why people perish?

Yes. It is not because God will not save people, or because Jesus did not die and open up a plain way of mercy for them, but because they refuse to be persuaded by the Holy Spirit to submit to God, give up their sins, and be saved.

> Yet you refuse to come to Me so that I can give you this eternal life. *(John 5:40 NLT)*
>
> Not at all! And you will also perish unless you turn from your evil ways and turn to God. *(Luke 13:3 NLT)*
>
> Anyone who believes and is baptized will be saved. But anyone who refuses to believe will be condemned. *(Mark 16:16 NLT)*

13. Then if I go to Hell, it is my own fault?

Yes, you will be forced to admit in the last day that God the Father loved and pitied you and made a way for your escape, that Jesus Christ died for you, that the Holy Spirit hounded you, and that it is all your own fault that you are not in heaven, among the blessed.

14. But how about those who have never heard the Gospel of Jesus?

Let's leave them to the mercy of God; it is sufficient for us to know that those who follow the light God gives them will, by virtue of the sacrifice of Jesus, be saved.

> The one who is the true light, who gives light to everyone, was going to come into the world. *(John 1:9 NLT)*

> Then Peter replied, "I see very clearly that God doesn't show partiality. In every nation He accepts those who fear Him and do what is right." *(Acts 10:34,35 NLT)*

15. So are the heathen in as good shape as those who have heard the Gospel?

Certainly not, because most don't "fear Him and do what is right" (as our Acts 10:34,35 text immediately above, requires). Therefore, it is our duty to get at them as quickly as possible.

16. So, are you saying that it is imperative for those who are saved to continually listen to the Holy Spirit and struggle with all of His power that works within us to overcome the opposition of sinners and bring them to God?

Definitely, and if we do not, we shall certainly be charged with the responsibility of their punishment. Oh, let us pray and preach, and visit and persuade people, so that, come judgment day, none of their blood will be on our skirts.

> But if the watchman sees the enemy coming and doesn't sound the alarm to warn the people, he is responsible for their deaths. They will die in their sins, but I will hold the watchman accountable. *(Ezekiel 33:6 NLT)*

> You can be sure that the one who brings that person back will save that sinner from death and bring about the forgiveness of many sins. *(James 5:20 NLT)*
>
> And then He told them, "Go into all the world and preach the Good News to everyone, everywhere." *(Mark 16:15 NLT)*

Reading Club Guide

How do you picture the Holy Spirit?

What important roles do you see Holy Spirit playing in salvation?

How do you hear Holy Spirit speaking directly to your heart?

---

[1] We should clarify. Originally, Booth used "Christ" instead of "Jesus." We want to avoid confusion about the divinity here. The question is asking if Holy Spirit was active in the world before Jesus was born on earth. Jesus is eternal. But Holy Spirit was active in the world before He was born in Bethlehem.

[2] This is what Booth writes. But maybe these Primitive Salvationist means of grace can serve a similar purpose for us today.

PART 1 | Section 10

Conditions of Salvation: Repentance and Faith

1. What are the conditions of salvation?

Repentance towards God and faith in our Lord Jesus Christ. The Gospel nutshell is "repent and believe."[1]

2. What is Repentance?

In true repentance—

i. You are convinced that you are a sinner in danger of Hell.

ii. You hate your sins.

iii. You are sorry you ever committed them.

iv. You want to stop committing them.

v. You want God to forgive you.

3. What do you mean that to get saved you have to be convinced of sinful guilt and the immi nence of eternity in Hell?

We mean that you see sin to be the evil thing which God hates, and which must be either forgiven or punished.

4. Are repenting converts always sorry for their sin?

Yes. If you truly repent, you always regret your wrongdoings. You are sorry and wish you had not acted so shamefully and ungratefully towards so loving a God.

5. Are such people always willing to give up sinning?

Yes. If you truly repent you are always willing, then and there, to renounce and give up forever the ways and doings that you regret. If you are not willing to give them up, you are a hypocrite. That repentance is hollow and useless if it doesn't sound like this: "God helping me, I will never do these things again."

6. What else does repentance mean?

The sinner who repents wants God to pardon him. It is the thought of forgiveness that is at the bottom of it all.

7. Can you be saved without first repenting?

Impossible! For God to forgive sinners without their repentance would do them a positive injury, and harden and encourage them in sin.

If children doing wrong are disobedient, play truant, or the like, do the parents at once forgive them, saying nothing about their sin? Of course not. If they did, the children would say, when tempted to do wrong again: Oh, my parents were not angry with us when we did wrong the other day—they did not punish us, but forgave us, and all went on a jolly as before. We can do the same things again, or anything else we like, and nothing unpleasant will happen. Oh, no, a wise parent would refuse to forgive and be reconciled to the children until they had repented, and promised not to offend again. And God acts in just the same way.

8. Then those people who say they are forgiven first and repent afterwards are deluded?

Yes, undoubtedly. It does not follow that they are not forgiven, but they mistake the order of the work in their own minds.

9. Do people often miss the difference between being willing to give up sin and having power to give it up?

Definitely. That's why it is so important to constantly emphasize this point with people. You may be willing to be saved from drowning by any means, and yet completely lack the power to save yourself. In the same way, you may be perfectly willing for God to save you in your own way, although perfectly sure of being unable to save yourself.

10. What is faith?

The faith that saves a sinner sounds like this: God has promised to forgive those who repent and come to Him through the blood of Jesus Christ, His Son. I repent and come to Him, trusting only in the blood of Jesus Christ for mercy, and I believe that He does now receive and forgive me.

> Jesus told her, "I am the resurrection and the life. Those who believe in Me, even though they die like everyone else, will live again." *(John 11:25 NLT)*

> I assure you, those who listen to My message and believe in God who sent Me have eternal life. They will never be condemned for their sins, but they have already passed from death into life. *(John 5:24 NLT)*

11. Describe Saving Faith further?

It speaks in this way — I believe that Christ loved me and died for me, that His death is the atonement for my sin, and I believe that His blood does now wash all my sins away.

12. Is everyone pardoned that comes to God in this way?

Yes, everyone who believes like this and repents of sin.

People who cover over their sins will not prosper. But if they confess and forsake them, they will receive mercy. *(Proverbs 2:13 NLT)*

Everyone who believes in me will have eternal life. *(John 3:15 NLT)*

There is no judgment awaiting those who trust Him. But those who do not trust Him have already been judged for not believing in the only Son of God. *(John 3:18 NLT)*

13. Then the death of Christ is the only ground of faith for a sinner before God?

Yes, although you repent and trust in God as directed, confidence is still based only and solely in the fact revealed to you in the Bible that Christ loved you and gave Himself for you.[2]

14. What does "declared righteous" mean?

But people are declared righteous because of their faith, not because of their work. *(Romans 4:5 NLT)*

And because of Abraham's faith, God declared him to be righteous. *(Romans 4:22 NLT)*

This expression simply means that lacking any righteousness in which to appear before God, He accepts our faith in Christ instead. That is, that as God treated Christ as the sinner for our sakes, so He treats those who believe on Him as though they were righteous for His sake.

15. Isn't there a deeper meaning than this?

Yes. These and similar passages also teach that faith is counted for righteousness, because it is God's means of actually *making* us righteous. In this sense we are justified, that is *made just by faith*.

Reading Club Guide

What part of the salvation process is often missing these days? Why?

How can we more comprehensively present the Gospel to individuals?

---

[1] Mark 1:15 NIV.

[2] Galatians 2:20

PART 1 | Section 11

The Forgiveness of Sins

1. We read much in the New Testament about being justified. What is justification?

Justification is God pardoning our sins for Jesus' sake and receiving us into His favor.[1]

2. Do pardon and justification mean the same blessing?

They do in the Bible when they refer to Salvation. But in different contexts they mean different things. For example: In a court of law to justify is to pronounce a person innocent because it is impossible to prove him guilty, while in the Gospel to justify is to deliver a person, admittedly guilty, by an act of pardon.

3. Do the Scriptures lump them together?

Yes.

> Brothers, listen! In this man Jesus there is forgiveness for your sins. Everyone who believes in Him is freed from all guilt and declared right with God—something the Jewish law could never do. *(Acts 13:38,39 NLT)*

4. When God forgives someone's sins, does He pardon all at once?

All at a stroke. It could not be otherwise. A *thorough* repentance brings a *complete* forgiveness.[2] The story of the Prodigal Son proves this, if it requires any proving. *(Luke 15)*

> I—yes, I alone—am the one who blots out your sins for My own sake and will never think of them again. *(Isaiah 43:25 NLT)*
>
> The LORD is merciful and gracious; He is slow to get angry and full of unfailing love. *(Psalm 53:8 NLT)*

5. What are the conditions of a sinner's justification before God?

Repentance and faith.[3]

6. What is the ground for a sinner's salvation?

The love of the Father, Son, and Holy Spirit, as displayed in the gift, suffering, and death of Jesus Christ.

7. Is Jesus any more the cause of salvation than Father God?

Certainly not. And it is false and unscriptural to represent the Son as loving us more than the Father does. The Godhead is involved in salvation: Son atones, Father forgives, Spirit regenerates. From our end, as the doctrine states, repentance toward God (the Father), faith in our Lord Jesus Christ and regeneration by the Holy Spirit are necessary to salvation.

8. When talking about the forgiveness of sins, is it wise to avoid such terms as regeneration, justification, and the like?

Use those terms that are in most people's vocabulary. If people understand regeneration, then use it. Otherwise, try plain words like forgiveness and conversion that people can understand.

Reading Club Guide

How are you justified?

On what basis can God forgive sins?

When did He forgive your sins?

How does it feel for you to have your sins forgiven?

[1] Justified, "made just by faith" (from section 10).

[2] We think it was William Sangster who taught that the blood only covers what we uncover.

[3] Mark 1:15; Acts 20:21; etc.

PART 1 | Section 12

Conversion

1. When God pardons a sinner, what other blessings follow?

He *converts* or *regenerates* him. He makes him a new creature.

What this means is that those who become Christians become new persons. They are not the same anymore, for the old life is gone. A new life has begun! *(2 Corinthians 5:17 NLT)*

2. Are regeneration and conversion basically the same?

Yes (but see points 3-6).

3. What is Conversion?

It is that change which God effects in you when He delivers you from the power and love of sin, and turns you round to love God and holiness and holy people. It is like being made over again, like becoming a new creation, like being born again.

4. Is this what Jesus meant when He said, "You must be born again?"

Yes. It is the soul starting life afresh, with new instincts, new aims, and new relationships. You have been brought into a new spiritual world with a new spiritual force within you, to live on new spiritual food, do new spiritual work, with new spiritual companions, and bound for a new spiritual home. It can be accurately said that you, having repented and believing, have become, "*a* new creation" *(2 Corinthians 5:17)*.

> He saved us, not because of the good things we did, but because of his mercy. He washed away our sins and gave us a new life through the Holy Spirit. *(Titus 3:5 NLT)*

5. Does regeneration completely transform you?

No, it is not normally complete, for there is still left hanging about the soul, and dwelling in it, many of the old evil tendencies which, although brought under subjection by divine grace, still often rise, overcome, and drag him into sin.[1] It certainly does change us, though.

6. What is the difference between justification and regeneration?

Justification is the pardon of sin. Regeneration is the changing of our nature.

Justification is an act of mercy that God performs for us. Regeneration is a work done within us.

Justification is a change of our relationship, when from being the children of the devil, we are made the children of God. Regeneration is a change of our character, in which we are transformed into goodness and truth and love after the likeness of God.

> Jesus replied, "I assure you, unless you are born again, you can never see the Kingdom of God." *(John 3:3 NLT)*
>
> It doesn't make any difference now whether we have been circumcised or not. What counts is whether we really have been changed into new and different people. *(Galatians 6:15 NLT)*

Reading Club Guide

How do you distinguish between regeneration and justification?

How do you distinguish between pardon and conversion?

How can we persuade more people to enjoy each of these experiences?

How does it feel for you to have your sins forgiven?

---

[1] See Romans 12:2; Ephesians 4:23; etc.

PART 1 | Section 13

The Two Natures

1. Don't many evangelists and others teach a view of regeneration quite different from that described in the last section?

Yes, they teach that in regeneration the natural, sinful people are not changed at all, that if they are naturally lying, thieving, adulterous spirits, they remain so to the end of life. But they hold that at conversion, to counteract and keep down this wicked nature, another spirit is put within each individual, which is good and incapable of either doing wrong or being destroyed. This new spirit or nature will live alongside the evil nature till death – sometimes being the master, and sometimes being mastered. Thus every saved person must have in them two natures.

[Ed. note, it is the last three sentences directly above that General Booth goes on to attack in the rest of this section, specifically, that 1. the good is incapable of being destroyed; 2. we're stuck with the evil nature 'til death; and, 3. all Christians have two natures. It is implicitly an argument for holiness.]

What text supports this view?

> It seems to be a fact of life that when I want to do what is right, I inevitably do what is wrong. *(Romans 7:21 NLT)*

2. How do you explain this passage?

It describes a convicted sinner's struggle, which, although awakened to feel the evil of sin and the attractiveness of Holiness, is stuck under the power of his sinful habits and inclinations. So, while he wants to follow the Spirit, his natural inclinations to sin hold him back, and lead him away in an opposite direction.[1]

3. Is this the only passage referenced to support this view?

No. Galatians 5:17 is also quoted as one of the strongest:

> The old sinful nature loves to do evil, which is just opposite from what the Holy Spirit wants. And the Spirit gives us desires that are opposite from what the sinful nature desires. These two forces are constantly fighting each other, and your choices are never free from this conflict. *(Galatians 5:17 NLT)*

But these Galatians were backsliding, as is clear from the preceding part of the chapter, and especially from the seventh verse. They had fallen back again into the powerless condition of convicted sinners, and therefore their unsanctified inclinations resisted the Spirit's working, and brought them again into bondage. What is noteworthy is that the Apostle doesn't accept this miserable experience as the proper condition of a saved man. Instead, he rebukes it, and goes on to show, in verses 24 and 25, that those who retain their union with Christ crucify the affections and lusts of the flesh, and live and walk in the power of the Spirit. Hallelujah!

[Ed. note, so, in this response, General Booth is allowing that these two texts – Galatians 5:17 and 5:24,25 - might also describe the experience of slacker Christians.]

How else can you show this doctrine to be false?

From consciousness. As a Christian (assuming you are a born again), you may sense that, on one hand you have inclinations to good, while on the other hand you have lingering tendencies toward evil. You're still one person. You don't have two distinct and separate natures. When you do good, you feel that you, a person, by God's grace, for His glory, have done it, and you sense some self-approving satisfaction. And if you do wrong (tell it not in Gath! Proclaim it not in the streets of Ashkelon!), you recognize that you, yourself, have done it, and you condemn yourself for it.

4. Is not common sense also against this doctrine?

Is this old nature physical, that is, a part of my body, or is it spiritual? If sin were in my body, that is, really and truly a part of my flesh, then the less there is of the body the better, for the less there is of the devilish to contend against. We should all go on diets to lose weight and weaken that physical sinful nature![2]

Again, if the body was essentially sinful how is it purified? Does death or the corruption of the grave destroy the sinful nature? If so, then death, and rottenness, and worms can do what Jesus' blood and the Holy Ghost cannot do.

If this old nature is not a physical body but a spirit, you've got as many difficulties, some of which are as follow:

i. If I have in me two natures, that is, two distinct spirits—one good and the other evil—one doing all the good that is done, and the other all the evil, which spirit am I? An individual person cannot be both natures at the same time. If I can, then there are two separate natures, as is contended, but only one, as we contend. But if they are distinct and separate, am I the bad spirit, or am I the good spirit?

ii. But if I am the bad spirit, or nature, how shall I get to Heaven? Because it, the old nature, we are told, can never be made good.

iii. If I am the good spirit, I am not responsible for the conduct of the bad nature; and if I steal, or lie, or commit adultery, it is not me that lies, or commits adultery, but the bad spirit that is in me, and I cannot help it, and ought not to be punished for it, either here or hereafter.

iv. If I am not the good spirit, and if I am not the bad spirit, then I must be a separate spirit, sometimes taking part with the good spirit, and sometimes being influenced by the bad one. If so, there must be three spirits, that is: first, I, myself; second, the spirit or nature, which came with my natural birth; and third, the new spirit, which came from God, at my second birth. This cannot be, because I feel and know that I am only one person, one spirit.

v. But further, supposing the evil spirit to be a separate nature, as it is stated, and a spiritual nature as it must be, what is to become of it at death? If I go to Heaven, where will it go?

Death cannot destroy it. Death has no power over the spirit, to refine or to kill. It cannot go into the grave. It cannot go into Heaven, because nothing unholy enters there. The advocates of this view deny the existence of purgatory, or it might be lodged there. And if it goes to Hell, a part of me will be in Hell, and a part in Heaven.

Common sense is against this argument.

5. Is the Bible against this doctrine of the two natures?

The practical parts of the Bible are against it: that is, all the commands, exhortations, warnings and promises of the Bible are addressed to the individual himself, and not to some separate spirit or nature in him. The Apostles continually addressed those to whom they wrote as "believers," "you," "everybody," "everyone," and so on, plainly showing that their exhortations were given to the persons themselves, and not to a distinct and separate something in them. Further, these exhortations would be unnecessary to the good nature, which is said to be incapable of sinning, and they would be useless to the bad nature, which is said to be incapable of being mended.

6. Does not this view destroy the practical application of the Atonement?

Yes, it sets aside the necessity for the application of the cleansing blood of Christ to the soul, seeing that the new nature is incapable of sinning, and therefore needs no cleansing, and the old nature is incapable of being cleansed.

7. Can you give me any passages from the Bible that are against this view?

Yes, any number, but specially all those texts which speak of the destruction of the old nature and of complete deliverance from the power and indwelling of sin.

[Ed. note, here, General Booth dismantles the arguments that we're stuck with the evil nature 'til death, and that every Christian must always have two natures.]

I myself no longer live, but Christ lives in me. So I live my life in this earthly body by trusting in the Son of God, who loved me and gave Himself for me. *(Galatians 2:20 NLT)*

That is, my old sinful self is put to death as truly as the body of Christ was crucified for me. How could Paul's sinful nature be crucified, and yet remain in full strength and vigor, only being kept down by another nature planted within him?

> Our old sinful selves were crucified with Christ so that sin might lose its power in our lives. We are no longer slaves to sin. *(Romans 6:6 NLT)*

If the body or substance of sin was destroyed, that they might not serve sin, how could it be in them unchanged and indestructible? This would be an absurdity.

> But if we confess our sins to him, He is faithful and

> just to forgive us and to cleanse us from every wrong. *(1 John 1:9 NLT)*

When God has cleansed a soul from all unrighteousness, how insulting it must be to Him for anyone to say that soul remains as sinful as ever.

> Now you are free from sin, your old master, and you have become slaves to your new master, righteousness. *(Romans 6:18 NLT)*

How can a man be made free from sin, empowered to serve righteousness, and at the same time be full of sin, and have in him a wicked, devilish nature, as those who hold these views say?

> Those who belong to Christ Jesus have nailed the passions and desires of their sinful nature to his cross and crucified them there. *(Galatians 5:24 NLT)*

Crucifying the affections and lusts must refer to a real, practical dying of all evil.

> But if we are living in the light of God's presence, just as Christ is, then we have fellowship with each other, and the blood of Jesus, His Son, cleanses us from every sin. *(1 John 1:7 NLT)*

> Then I will sprinkle clean water on you, and you will be clean. Your filth will be washed away, and you will no longer worship idols. *(Ezekiel 36:25 NLT)*

How can a soul be cleansed from all its filthiness, and from all its idols, and still be as dirty and idolatrous as ever? If Christians had dealt with other parts of the Bible as they have with these and similar texts, we might as well never have had any Bible.

Reading Club Guide

Can you relate with the dreadful experience of constant Christian failure?

Have you any ideas as to how to win victory over this experience? (This important subject will be covered in chapters to follow.)

---

[1] Another take on Romans 7 is that it reflects the frustration of trying to keep the Mosaic law without the power of the Holy Spirit (God-fearing Jews being the group to which Paul used to belong).

[2] Our language limits us here. Though Paul talks of sinful nature (Romans 7:5,18,25; 8:3,4,5,6,8,9…) and teaches that our old sinful selves are crucified (Romans 6:6) we afterwards still have a "nature." The term isn't helpful in this situation. We suggest substituting "natural inclination to act selfishly."

PART 1 | Section 14

Assurance

1. If you are saved will you know it?

Yes, unquestionably.

2. How do you respond to someone asking for proof that God assures those He saves that they actually are saved?

I should say—

i. I know it.

ii. The Bible shows that the Prophets and Apostles and Saints knew it. Job knew that "his Redeemer lived." Enoch knew that he pleased God. Nothing in the Bible is more evident than that those holy people acted, fought, and suffered under the fullest conviction that they were the children and servants of the Most High God. It is ridiculous to suppose that Hebrews 11 could be true of any but those who were as confident of the friendship and fatherhood of God as they were of anything else.

It is by our actions that we know we are living in the truth, so we will be confident when we stand before the Lord. *(1 John 3:19 NLT)*

iii. The Bible says this is the common experience of Christians.

And because you Gentiles have become His children, God has sent the Spirit of His Son into your hearts, and now you can call God your dear Father. *(Galatians 4:6 NLT)*

iv. Common sense says that you could not be forgiven—be made a new creature, love God with all your heart, give up living a selfish, devilish life, have a heart washed from sin, consecrate yourself to soul-saving, and, altogether, live such a Christ-like life as someone must live to be a Christian—and yet be in doubt all the time whether or not such a change had taken place in you.

3. But how do you know that you are saved?

i. You remember the time when and the place where God saved you.

ii. You know you live a converted life—walk, talk, pray, fight, love, and hate like a saved person. "He hates the things that before he loved, and loves the things that before he hated," and therefore you know you are a new creature, and, knowing that nothing short of the power of God could effect this change, you conclude that you have been converted.

iii. But further and more convincing still to you, you feel that you are saved.

If someone was to ask you how you knew that you had a natural life, you might say—

(a) I can perform such acts as only a living person can perform.
(b) I feel I am alive.

Just so here. Not only can you do such works as only a saved person can but you feel that you are saved—you know it. This is the shortest and most convincing proof.

4. What do you call this feeling?

Assurance. The Assurance of Salvation.

5. How is assurance produced?

Assurance emerges from the revelation of forgiveness and acceptance, made by God Himself directly to your soul. This is the witness of the Spirit. It is God, testifying in my soul that He has loved me, and given Himself for me, and washed me from my sins in His own blood. Nothing short of this actual revelation, made by God Himself, can make anyone sure of salvation. Assurance is founded upon the promises of God in Scripture *(such as Romans 8:15-17; Galatians 4:6; 1 Thessalonians 1:5; Colossians 2:2; John 5:24; 1 John 5:10-13)*.

6. But aren't there many sincere followers of God who are unsure of salvation?

Yes, because they are not saved. If they get properly saved they will have the joy and witness and power of it. Still, there are doubtless many who have never come to understand that they can be saved, who, as soon as they hear the amazing good news, press into the kingdom.

7. What is adoption?

The act by which God introduces pardoned, regenerated rebels into His family, and makes them His sons and daughters.

> And since we are His children, we will share His treasures-for everything God gives to His Son, Christ, is ours, too. But if we are to share His glory, we must also share His suffering. *(Romans 8:17 NLT)*

Reading Club Guide

Are you saved?

How do you know you are saved?

How has this chapter helped give you assurance of your salvation?

PART 1 | Section 15

Sanctification. What it is.

1. What does the Army teach on the subject of entire sanctification?

That you may be delivered from all sin, and enabled to do the will of God continually in this life.

> We have been rescued from our enemies, so we can serve God without fear, in holiness and righteousness forever. *(Luke 1:74,75 NLT)*

2. What is sin?

Narrowly defined, sin consists in doing that which we know to be wrong, inwardly or outwardly, or in not doing that which we know to be right.[1]

> Those who sin are opposed to the law of God, for all sin opposes the law of God. *(1 John 3:4 NLT)*
>
> Remember, it is sin to know what you ought to do and then not do it. *(James 4:17 NLT)*
>
> Every wrong is sin. *(1 John 5:17 NLT)*

3. Can sin be spoken of both as an ACT and as a PRINCIPLE?

Yes, in the same way that you can speak of the fruit and the root of a tree. Sin, as an act, is the fruit: as a principle, it is the root.

4. What are doubtful actions?

Doubtful actions are those about the rightness or wrongness of which we lack biblically based confidence of faith.

5. Are doubtful actions sinful?

Yes, The Bible represents them as such.

> If you do anything you believe is not right, you are sinning. *(Romans 14:23b NLT)*

You may have the faith to believe that there is nothing wrong with what you are doing, but keep it between yourself and God. Blessed are those who do not condemn themselves by doing something they know is all right. *(Romans 14:22 NLT)*

6. What is sanctification?

Sanctification is the separation of the soul from sin, and the devotion of the whole being to the will and service of God.

> You can be sure of this: The LORD has set apart the godly for Himself. The LORD will answer when I call to Him. *(Psalm 4:3 NLT)*

> But the person who is joined to the Lord becomes one spirit with Him. *(1 Corinthians 6:17 NLT)*

7. Can sanctification be partial? And can it be complete?

Yes. It is partial in nearly everyone when first converted, and entire when they are "fully saved" or made holy.

> Look after each other so that none of you will miss out on the special favor of God. Watch out that no bitter root of unbelief rises up among you, for whenever it springs up; many are corrupted by its poison. *(Hebrews 12:15 NLT)*

8. What is partial sanctification?

It is being delivered from the power of sin, and yet having sin existing in the soul; sin is there, but it does not reign.

> I couldn't talk to you as I would to mature Christians. I had to talk as though you belonged to this world or as though you were infants in the Christian life. *(1 Corinthians 3:1 NLT)*

9. What is the difference partial sanctification and pre-conversion?

Partial sanctification is described in point 8. When in the state of pre-conversion, you are actually under the power and dominion of sin. You may see it to be evil, hate it, and struggle against it, but you are still under its power and forced to obey it. For instance, see how some people make resolutions and break them directly. They cannot help but sin, though a truly converted person has power over sin, but the root or the principle of sin is still in his soul.

> The law is good, then. The trouble is not with the law but with me, because I am sold into slavery, with sin as my master. I don't understand myself at all, for I really want to do what is right, but I don't do it. Instead, I do the very thing I hate. *(Romans 7:14,15 NLT)*

> Sin is no longer your master, for you are no longer subject to the law, which enslaves you to sin. Instead, you are free by God's grace. *(Romans 6:14 NLT)*

10. What is entire sanctification?

Entire sanctification is complete deliverance from sin. The natural inclination to act selfishly is removed from the soul, and all the powers, faculties, possessions, and influences of the soul are given up to the service and glory of God.

> But now you are free from the power of sin and have become slaves of God. Now you do those things that lead to holiness and result in eternal life. *(Romans 6:22 NLT)*

11. Then people in the three conditions named stand in three distinct relationships to sin?

Yes—that is to say—

i. They can be under sin. *(Romans 7:14)*

ii. They can be over sin. *(Romans 6:14)*

iii. They can be without sin. *(Romans 6:7)*

12. Will you explain this further?

i. In an unconverted state they are under sin.

ii. In a justified state they are over sin.

iii. In an entirely sanctified state they are without sin.[2]

13. Does the Army teach sinless perfection?

Certainly not.

14. What is sinless perfection?

This would be similar to Adam's experience before he first sinned—he was perfect and able to perfectly obey the perfect law of God.

15. Is it possible to attain to sinless perfection in this life?

No! An imperfect creature cannot perfectly obey a perfect law, and people, being imperfect both in body and in mind, are plainly unable to keep the perfect law of God.

16. Does God require that we obey a law He knows it is impossible to obey?

No. We cannot imagine a benevolent Being requiring from us that which is impossible, and then condemning us for not doing it. His service is a reasonable service, and His commandments are not grievous *(1 John 5:3; Romans 12:1)*.[3]

17. What, then, is the law that He expects us to keep?

The law of love, as laid down and described by Jesus Christ, when He said: "Love the Lord thy God with all your heart," or in other words, love and serve God according to your knowledge and ability, and He will be satisfied.

> You must love the Lord your God with all your heart, all your soul, and all your mind. *(Matthew 22:37 NLT)*
>
> Then Peter replied, "I see very clearly that God doesn't show partiality. In every nation He accepts those who fear Him and do what is right." *(Acts 10:34,35 NLT)*

18. When we talk of sanctification, or being sanctified, do we not generally mean entire sanctification?

Yes, and we also mean the same experience by such terms as Perfect Love, or Holiness, or the Blessing, or Full Salvation, or a Clean Heart, and the like.

19. If someone is entirely sanctified, is this person delivered from temptation?

No! Adam and Eve were tempted, and so was Jesus Christ, and they were holy, and the holier a man becomes, the more likely Satan is to tempt you. Holiness does not bring freedom from temptation, but victory over it.

> God blesses the people who patiently endure testing. Afterward they will receive the crown of life that God has promised to those who love Him. *(James 1:12 NLT)*

20. Does sanctification mean that we are saved from mistakes in judgment?

No! That would be making us infallible. Still, sanctified people are promised, and do enjoy, the direct guidance of the Holy Spirit: they acknowledge Him in all their ways, and He directs their paths.

> But when the Father sends the Counselor as My representative—and by the Counselor I mean the Holy Spirit—He will teach you everything and will remind you of everything I myself have told you. *(John 14:26 NLT)*

21. Does holiness save people from physical and mental frailty?

No, but it frequently leads to a fuller sanctification of all the affliction and infirmities from which saints suffer, and often to the exercise of faith for their deliverance.

> And their prayer offered in faith will heal the sick, and the Lord will make them well. And anyone who has committed sins will be forgiven. *(James 5:15 NLT)*

22. Does sanctification make backsliding impossible?

No. Satan fell from Heaven and Adam from Paradise, and they both were perfect, in a sense in which we never can be in this life. And we do not see any state of grace revealed in the Bible as attainable in this life from which it is not possible to fall.

> It isn't my responsibility to judge outsiders, but it certainly is your job to judge those inside the church who are sinning in these ways. *(1 Corinthians 5:12 NLT)*

> What I say to you I say to everyone: Watch for His return! *(Mark 13:37 NLT)*[4]

23. Does sanctification make spiritual growth impossible?

No! Sanctification means the cleansing of the heart from pride and unbelief and all other native evils, and so makes growth in grace certain and easy—just as the pulling up of the weeds in the garden is favorable to the growth, strength, and fruitfulness of the garden's plants.

Reading Club Guide

What is sanctification? Is it possible?

What God command, God enables. How does that affect your response to His holiness commands?

Are you experiencing what this chapter explains?

---

[1] John Wesley defines "sin properly so-called" as a voluntary transgression of a known law of God, and understands that freedom from this sin as characteristic of biblical holiness.

[2] The proof-text rebuttal of 1 John 1:8 ignores that context, specifically verses 7 and 9 ("cleanse us from every sin/wrong"). Booth is not asserting sinlessness from birth but a sin-free experience as outlined in 1 John 1:7,9.

[3] Our premise is that God is not mean-spirited. If He did command us to do that which is impossible, then He is bound to punish us for our inevitable disobedience. Such action would expose Him as mean-spirited. The principle behind our discussion is that what God commands, God enables.

[4] See also verses such as Proverbs 4:23; Matthew 5:13; John 15:6; Galatians 5:4; Luke 9:62; 8:32; Hebrews 6:4-6; 2 Peter 2:20-22; etc. on backsliding in general. Final salvation is promised to those who endure to the end (see Colossians 1:22,23; Hebrews 3:14; 10:38-39; Jude 20,21; Matthew 10:22; 24:13; Revelation 2:10). See also section 22 in part 1 of this book.

PART 1 | Section 16

Sanctification. Can it be attained?

1. What do Christians who disagree with you on this subject deny about this experience?

They assert that we cannot be holy during our lives and that we must continue sinning and confessing, sinning and confessing until we die. But they still believe that somehow we have to be sanctified, somewhere between death and entering heaven.

2. How can you prove that this holiness may be enjoyed in this life?

Our first argument is from probability. It seems most likely that God should provide for the immediate and entire deliverance of people from sin. If your child was poisoned, we are all sure that you would use every means, as soon as possible, not only to get a portion, but all of the poison drawn out. In the same way, we think it most likely that God would use all possible means to get all of the deadly poison of sin out of your soul.

3. If that is so, then, some might ask, why doesn't God save His people from all their troubles?

Nice, but this is an entirely different thing. Trouble is not always injurious to you. In fact, it is often a blessing to those who love God. On the contrary, sin is evil, always evil, hateful to God, and a curse to those stuck in it.

4. How else can you prove that God wants to save us from all sin in this life?

The Bible is about as clear as it gets on this subject. These verses describe in various ways that holiness is the possible experience of the saints:

i. As a clean heart—that is, a heart washed from all sin.

   Create in me a clean heart, O God. Renew a right spirit within me. *(Psalm 51:10 NLT)*

   God blesses those whose hearts are pure, for they will see God. *(Matthew 5:8 NLT)*

   The purpose of my instruction is that all the Christians there would be filled with love that comes from a pure heart, a clear conscience, and sincere faith. *(1 Timothy 1:5 NLT)*

ii. A heart delivered from all idolatry.

   Then I will sprinkle clean water on you, and you will be clean. Your filth will be washed away, and you will no longer worship idols. *(Ezekiel 36:25 NLT)*

iii. As being altogether separated from evil and devoted to God.

Now may the God of peace make you holy in every way, and may your whole spirit and soul and body be kept blameless until that day when our Lord Jesus Christ comes again. *(1 Thessalonians 5:23 NLT)*

iv. As living such a blameless life that God Himself shall not see anything to condemn.

Your attitude should be the same that Christ Jesus had. *(Philippians 2:15 NLT)*

He will keep you strong right up to the end, and He will keep you free from all blame on the great day when our Lord Jesus Christ returns. *(1 Corinthians 1:8 NLT)*

v. As being wholly devoted to God to be possessed and used by Him.

And so, dear brothers and sisters, I plead with you to give your bodies to God. Let them be a living and holy sacrifice—the kind He will accept. *(Romans 12:1 NLT)*

vi. As fulfilling the law.

Love does no wrong to anyone, so love satisfies all of God's requirements. *(Romans 13:10 NLT)*

vii. It is described as perfection (that is, perfection in love).

But you are to be perfect, even as your Father in heaven is perfect. *(Matthew 5:48 NLT)*

That is, if we are fully devoted to lives of love and goodness in our sphere, and according to our ability, as our Heavenly Father is in His sphere, we shall be perfect before Him.

It is God's way of preparing us in every way, fully equipped for every good thing God wants us to do. *(2 Timothy 3:17 NLT)*

He always prays earnestly for you, asking God to make you strong and perfect, fully confident of the whole will of God. *(Colossians 4:12 NLT)*

viii. As following the Lord fully. Joshua and Caleb did this, and went into Canaan.

But my servant Caleb is different from the others. He has remained loyal to me, and I will bring him into the land he explored. His descendants will receive their full share of that land. *(Numbers 14:24 NLT)*

ix. As being dead to sin; as having the old man crucified (that is, slain): as being freed from sin: as being alive to God.

I myself no longer live, but Christ lives in me. So I live my life in this earthly body by trusting in the Son of God, who loved me and gave Himself for me. *(Galatians 2:20 NLT)*

Old sinful selves were crucified with Christ so that sin might lose its power in our lives. We are no longer slaves to sin. For when we died with Christ we were set free from the power of sin. *(Romans 6:6,7 NLT)*

x. As being made altogether good.

A tree is identified by its fruit. Make a tree good, and its fruit will be good. Make a tree bad, and its fruit will be bad. *(Matthew 12:33 NLT)*

We can say with confidence and a clear conscience that we have been honest and sincere in all our dealings. We have depended on God's grace, not on our own earthly wisdom. That is how we have acted toward everyone, and especially toward you. *(2 Corinthians 1:12 NLT)*

Because of this, I always try to maintain a clear conscience before God and everyone else. *(Acts 24:16 NLT)*

As for me, God forbid that I should boast about anything except the cross of our Lord Jesus Christ. Because of that cross, my interest in this world died long ago, and the world's interest in me is also long dead. (*Galatians 6:14 NLT)*

xi. As being filled with the Spirit, and fully equipped for service.

Dear brothers and sisters, pattern your lives after mine, and learn from those who follow our example. *(Philippians 3:17 NLT)*

But we are citizens of heaven, where the Lord Jesus Christ lives. And we are eagerly waiting for Him to return as our Savior. *(Philippians 3:20 NLT)*

No eye has seen, no ear has heard, and no mind has imagined what God has prepared those who love Him. But we know these things because God has revealed them to us by His Spirit, and His Spirit searches out everything and shows us even God's deep secrets. *(1 Corinthians 2:9,10 NLT)*

May you experience the love of Christ, though it is so great you will never fully understand it. Then you will be filled with the fullness of life and power that comes from God. *(Ephesians 3:19 NLT)*

xii. As being made to resemble the character of the blessed God Himself.

And as we live in God, our love grows more perfect. So we will not be afraid on the day of judgment, but we can face Him with confidence because we are like Christ here in this world. *(1 John 4:17 NLT)*

Reading Club Guide

Which of the dozen arguments is most persuasive to you? Why?

Which of the Bible verses is most helpful? Why?

Have you attained sanctification yet?

PART 1 | Section 17

Sanctification. It can be attained!

1. How else does the Bible teach that you can be holy in this life?

The Bible promises holiness to those who seek it.

> But if we confess our sins to Him, He is faithful and just to forgive us and to cleanse us from every wrong. *(1 John 1:9 NLT)*

> And now, may the God of peace, who brought again from the dead our Lord Jesus, equip you with all you need for doing His will. May He produce in you, through the power of Jesus Christ, all that is pleasing to Him. Jesus is the great Shepherd of the sheep by an everlasting covenant, signed with His blood. To Him be glory forever and ever. Amen. *(Hebrews 13:20,21 NLT)*

> Because we have these promises, dear friends, let us cleanse ourselves from everything that can defile our body or spirit. And let us work toward complete purity because we fear God. *(2 Corinthians 7:1 NLT)*

2. How else does the Bible suggest that this experience is attainable?

The Bible commands God's people to be holy.

> But now you must be holy in everything you do, just as God—who chose you to be His children—is holy. For He himself has said, "You must be holy because I am holy." *(1 Peter 1:15,16 NLT)*
>
> My dear children, I am writing this to you so that you will not sin. But if you do sin, there is someone to plead for you before the Father. He is Jesus Christ, the one who pleases God completely. *(1 John 2:1 NLT)*
>
> Throw off your old evil nature and your former way of life, which is rotten through and through, full of lust and deception. You must display a new nature because you are a new person, created in God's likeness—righteous, holy, and true. *(Ephesians 4:22,24)*
>
> He died once to defeat sin, and now He lives for the glory of God. So you should consider yourselves dead to sin and able to live for the glory of God through Christ Jesus. *(Romans 6:10,11 NLT)*

3. How else does the Bible show that we can be entirely sanctified?

Jesus Christ and the inspired writers of the Bible pray that saints should be holy.

> Make them pure and holy by teaching them Your words of truth. *(John 17:17 NLT)*

4. In what other way does the Bible insist on entire sanctification?

The Bible declares that salvation from sin is the purpose of the life and death of Jesus Christ.

> And she will have a son, and you are to name Him Jesus, for He will save His people from their sins. *(Matthew 1:21 NLT)*
>
> He gave His life to free us from every kind of sin, to cleanse us, and to make us His very own people, totally committed to doing what is right. *(Titus 2:14 NLT)*
>
> Just think how much more the blood of Christ will purify our hearts from deeds that lead to death so that we can worship the living God. For by the power of the eternal Spirit, Christ offered himself to God as a perfect sacrifice for our sins. *(Hebrews 9:14 NLT)*
>
> But when people keep on sinning, it shows they belong to the devil, who has been sinning since the beginning. But the Son of God came to destroy these works of the devil. *(1 John 3:8 NLT)*
>
> He gave up his life for her ('the church') to make her holy and clean .... He did this to present her to Himself as a glorious church without a spot or wrinkle or any other blemish. Instead, she will be holy and without fault. *(Ephesians 5:25-27 NLT)*

5. Have you any more arguments to show that God's people can be pure in heart in this life?

Yes. The experience of God's people shows this.

6. Can you name any Bible characters who apparently enjoyed this experience?

Yes. Enoch and Moses and Job and many others, but we simply name the Apostle Paul, and give his experience in his own words.

> For to me, living is for Christ, and dying is even better. *(Philippians 1:21 NLT)*
>
> And you should follow my example, just as I follow Christ's. *(1 Corinthians 11:1 NLT)*
>
> You yourselves are our witnesses—and so is God—that we were pure and honest and faultless toward all of you believers. *(1 Thessalonians 2:10 NLT)*
>
> As for me, my life has already been poured out as an offering to God. The time of my death is near. I have fought a good fight, I have finished the race, and I have remained faithful. And now the prize awaits me—the crown of righteousness that the Lord, the righteous Judge, will give me on that great day of his return. And the prize is not just for me but for all who eagerly look forward to his glorious return. *(2 Timothy 4:6-8 NLT)*

7. Do you have any other argument to prove the possibility of enjoying this experience?

Yes. We think that all Christians will admit that in those moments when they realize the greatest intimacy with God they feel the strongest urgings of the Spirit to present their bodies as a living sacrifice, holy and acceptable to God.

Reading Club Guide

How does this chapter increase your hunger for this experience?

Can you name any other people (biblical or otherwise) who have experienced it?

How are/were they different than most Christians?

PART 1 | Section 18

Sanctification. The Conditions.

1. What are the conditions of entire sanctification?

Conviction, renunciation, consecration, and faith.

2. Explain the first.

By conviction for the blessing, we mean you must feel that you need to be holy. You must see how despicable the sin that lingers within you really is, from which God wants to deliver you. You must be convinced, also, that, if you seek deliverance with all your heart, you will find it. When you see that you need the blessing, and that you can actually obtain and enjoy it, you will now seek it with all your heart.

3. What is the second condition of sanctification?

The renunciation, or giving up, of all known evil and of everything that seems doubtful. You have to be willing to get rid of, forever, each and every thing that you know in your heart to be wrong or that you have any good reason to fear is not right.[1]

4. Should you tell people who want to be holy but who smoke or drink that they should quit cold-turkey?

Yes, because in this age, especially in the Army, few, if any, can smoke or drink without feeling both to be wasteful, injurious, and unclean habits. If they feel them such, or have even a question about their lawfulness, the indulgence must be given up at once. For whoever doubts is condemned.

5. Are there any Scripture passages showing these habits to be wrong, and altogether unworthy of a follower of Christ?

Yes, any number. We give two, but the whole tenor of Scripture, and the whole spirit of Christianity, is against them.

> Therefore, come out from them and separate yourselves from them, says the Lord. Don't touch their filthy things, and I will welcome you. And I will be your Father, and you will be my sons and daughters, says the Lord Almighty. *(2 Corinthians 6:17,18 NLT)*

> Go now; leave your bonds and slavery. Put Babylon behind you, with everything it represents, for it is unclean to you. You are the LORD's holy people. Purify yourselves, you who carry home the vessels of the LORD. *(Isaiah 52:11 NLT)*

6. Do you think that a person seeking the blessing should be willing to give up flashy and fashionable clothes?

Yes. All who desire to walk closely with the Lord must have serious misgivings about superfluous and unnecessary adornment; and, if you have a serious misgiving about the lawfulness of any habit, you can't embrace it without condemnation, and, whether it be in clothing, or business, or family arrangements, or anything else, if there is reason to think it wrong and displeasing to God, you must give it up.

7. Are there any Scriptures suggesting that God dislikes immodest clothing?

> Next the LORD will judge the women of Jerusalem, who walk around with their noses in the air, with tinkling ornaments on their ankles. Their eyes rove among the crowds, flirting with the men. The Lord will send a plague of scabs to ornament their heads. Yes, the LORD will make them bald for all to see! *(Isaiah 3:16,17 NLT)*

> And I want women to be modest in their appearance. They should wear decent and appropriate clothing and not draw attention to themselves by the way they fix their hair or by wearing gold or pearls or expensive clothes. For women who claim to be devoted to God should make themselves attractive by the good things they do. *(1 Timothy 2:9,10 NLT)*

[Ed. note, in these two responses, Booth is emphasizing the need for modesty in dress and attitude. He's not necessarily saying that you cannot pick up a great bargain at the Salvo Thrift Store that still looks good.]

Aren't we responsible for the influence that our habits of eating, drinking, dressing, and other things exert for good or evil upon those around us?

Yes, we are. The Bible is pretty clear on our responsibility to renounce not only those things and habits which are wrong in themselves, but also those things or habits that, though innocent, and, perhaps, harmless to us, are calculated to be harmful to others.

> But you must be careful with this freedom of yours. Do not cause a brother or sister with a weaker conscience to stumble... So because of your superior knowledge, a weak Christian, for whom Christ died, will be destroyed... If what I eat is going to make another Christian sin, I will never eat meat again as long as I live—for I don't want to make another Christian stumble. *(1 Corinthians 8:9,11, and 13 NLT)*
>
> Don't eat meat or drink wine or do anything else if it might cause another Christian to stumble. *(Romans 14:21 NLT)*
>
> Whatever you eat or drink or whatever you do, you must do all for the glory of God. *(1 Corinthians 10:31 NLT)*

Reading Club Guide

What changes when someone gets sanctified?

Of those discussed, what is the most difficult thing for you to give up? Why?

At what point does our responsibility to others end?

---

[1] Renunciation opens the door to deliverance from spiritual bondage. Once we renounce sin, evil spirits no longer have legal right to harass us and we can authoritatively expel them in Jesus' name.

PART 1 | Section 19

Sanctification. The Conditions (Consecration).

1. What is the third condition of entire sanctification?

The actual present surrender to God of our whole selves and all we possess.

2. Please explain.

Yes, gladly, as there are more serious mistakes made on this point than on any other in Christianity.

3. To help show what true consecration or surrender is, please describe Adam's behavior that made it all necessary.

Adam abandoned a life of entire and constant service to God, and set up one conveniently independent of Him. Adam ceased being a servant of Yahweh, and went, as they say, into business on his own account, as his own boss. He gave up living to please God in everything, and started to live to please himself.[1]

4. So, how do we, negatively affected by Adam's fallen condition, position ourselves in that place of God's confidence and favor which Adam abandoned?

Stop living independently of God. Stop living for your own pleasure and profit. Return to God. Lay everything that you are and all that you possess at Yahweh's feet, and offer to live completely to please and profit Him.

5. At what point do most people go astray on consecration?

It is not a reality to them. They pretend to give God all—their children, money, and possessions; their time and reputation; but it is only in imagination, in sentiment. It is not real. God and His cause are no better off after it than they were before, and the next day these people, who said at the mercy seat the previous night that they gave all they had to God, go about acting on the principle that all they have is their own, to be spent for their own pleasure, and their own profit, just as they did before.

6. Can you illustrate the kind of consecration—that is to say, the surrender—God wants?

A long time back, in England, there was a war between the king and the parliament, and the greater part of the nation took the side of the parliament, and the king was sorely pressed. It was then no uncommon thing for some nobleman or rich person to come in to the king and say, "I am sorry and ashamed that your majesty should be driven from your throne, and be suffering all this indignity and disgrace, and I want to help your majesty to get your rights again; and I have come with my sons and my servants to place our swords and our lives at your disposal. I have also mortgaged my estate and sold my plate, and brought the proceeds to help your majesty to carry on the war." Now, that was a real surrender, or giving up to that king: it was the laying of life and substance at his feet. If things went well with the king, it would be well with them, but if not, if the king lost all, they lost everything with him.

Now, that is just the kind of consecration God wants—only, one that goes deeper down still. He has been driven from His throne in the hearts of people everywhere, His name is cast out as evil, and people universally refuse to have Him to reign over them. Now, Jesus Christ wants to secure the Kingdom for His Father, and appeals for true-hearted soldiers who will help Him to succeed in this great undertaking, and He wants you to come into the camp in the same spirit that these old nobles did to their earthly king when he was in those desperate straits—to come, saying, "I bring my goods, my influence, my reputation, my family—aye, my life. I will have no separate interests: use all I have and am to promote the war, so that my King shall have His own, and His throne shall be established." That is consecration in reality, and only that. This is what Jesus Christ taught when He said, "Seek first the kingdom of God." This is what Jesus Christ exemplified in His life and death. This is what Paul and the first Apostles did, and if you are to be a thorough Christian, you must be consecrated in the same way.

> Or don't you know that your body is the temple of the Holy Spirit, who lives in you and was given to you by God? You do not belong to yourself, for God bought you with a high price. So you must honor God with your body. *(1 Corinthians 6:19,20 NLT)*

7. Then a true consecration, or surrender, has in it the nature of sacrifice?

Definitely. It is a real sacrifice. You present and give away all you have to God; you cease to own anything that has in the past been called your own. It all goes to God for His ordering and arranging. We position ourselves as servants, and receive back what He chooses. This, obviously, is no easy exercise, and can be accomplished only under the power of the Holy Spirit. But when all is laid on the altar—body, soul, spirit, possessions, reputation, all, all, all—then the fire descends and reduces all the dross and defilement to ashes, and fills your soul with burning zeal and blazing love and sizzling power.

> And so, dear brothers and sisters, I plead with you to give your bodies to God. Let them be a living and holy sacrifice—the kind He will accept. When you think of what He has done for you, is this too much to ask? Don't copy the behavior and customs of this world, but let God transform you into a new person by changing the way you think. Then you will know what God wants you to do, and you will know how good and pleasing and perfect His will really is. *(Romans 12:1,2 NLT)*

8. Is true consecration closely related with crucifixion?

Yes, undoubtedly, it is a real crucifixion. Crucifixion was a humiliating, painful death, and consecration means dying to all those pleasures and gratifications which flow from the improper love of self, the admiration of the world, the ownership of goods, and the inordinate love of family and friends, which go together to make up the life and joy of independent people (those who do not depend on Jesus). To do this is always a painful task, and yet we must be crucified with Christ if we are to live with Him.

> I myself no longer live, but Christ lives in me. So I live my life in this earthly body by trusting in the Son of God, who loved me and gave Himself for me. *(Galatians 2:20 NLT)*

> As for me, God forbid that I should boast about anything except the cross of our Lord Jesus Christ. Because of that cross, my interest in this world died long ago, and the world's interest in me is also long dead. *(Galatians 6:14 NLT)*

9. How do you give all of your property and money to God?

We think you should use your money and property to advance the kingdom in the way that God, from day to day, directs you, in the way most likely to accomplish that end. If the interests of the kingdom will be best served by selling your property, liquidating your assets and using this capital right away, then sell, liquidate and deploy that money. If the Lord shows you that you can help Christ's work better by retaining and using the income derived from it, then retain it and use the interest thereof.

10. What is the fourth condition?

Faith or trust. Sanctification is received by faith in the same way as forgiveness of sins.

11. What is the faith that sanctifies?

It is that act of simple trust which, on the authority of Christ's Word, says, "The blood of Jesus Christ does now cleanse me from all inward sin, and makes me pure in heart before Him; and I do here and now commit myself to Him, believing that He receives me, and that He will evermore keep me holy while I so trust Him."

12. When people trust God to that end, will they be, in every case, made clean?

Yes, always. If you, assured that you fully renounce all known and doubtful wrong-doing, and submitted to God's will in all things, are trusting God for full cleansing, you have the authority of God's Word to support your belief that the work is done, no matter how you feel. And you must hold on to this faith until the feeling comes.

> If we confess our sins to Him, He is faithful (to His own promise) and just (to the suffering and agony of His Son, which purchased the blessing) to forgive us and to cleanse us from every wrong. *(1 John 1:9 NLT)*

13. What do you mean by 'holding on until the feeling comes'?

Sometimes, God tests faith for a little time, and although you know that you put your sacrifice on the altar—that you are fully consecrated, and have the witness in yourself, the Holy Spirit's confirmation, that you believe that God accepts it; still, you may have to wait, like Abraham did, for the fire.[2] The fire confirms your inward feeling and faith in God's cleansing, and, if you watch your sacrifice, and wait a season, consumes it.

14. Is it right to tell people seeking purity that if they believe that the cleansing work is done it is done?

No, though there is a tension in points 13 and 14, it is right, and there is authority in the Bible, and in the experiences of God's people, for believing that if you trust God for the cleansing application of the precious blood, having fulfilled the previous conditions, God will, in the moment that faith is exercised, work the blessed change, and give the staying power.

15. Don't many seek this blessing without finding it?

Yes, multitudes do, and then, because they do not find it, they go around saying it is not attainable.

16. Why do so many seek and not find?

In general, it is because they do not seek this kingdom of God with all their hearts.

17. Is it because many refuse to fully surrender that they fail to obtain the blessing?

Yes. They go on well until they come to the point where they have to make the sacrifice of some darling idol, or where they see it will interfere with their reputation, or where they see it means selling all they have to help forward the kingdom, then they hesitate, refuse, and go away sorrowful—in many instances, it is to be feared, to declension and backsliding.

18. Do many stumble at the simplicity of faith?

Yes. We expect that many people who actually consecrate themselves and are willing to follow the Lamb wherever He leads fall short when it comes to believing that God does, there and then, cleanse them. They are always coming up to the edge of the cleansing wave, stripped and ready for the sanctifying plunge, but, tragically, they do not step in.

19. Don't many say that they do believe, and yet do not get any further?

Yes, they say they believe, and they do believe something about God's willingness or ability, but they do not believe that God does, really and truly, at this moment cleanse; and you must press them to this, drive them up to it. And when they do really trust God for a "full salvation," you will see the difference in them.

20. Aren't some holiness seekers hindered by looking at their feelings?

Yes, they are, and you must always be on your watch against this hindrance as well. Get them off from looking at themselves and their feelings to looking to God. You cannot too plainly and repeatedly press upon their attention that it is God that saves: that their work is to trust God, and that it is God's work to save them—that they must believe first, and feel afterwards.

21. Is it important to clearly understand that it is God who cleanses, and that faith and consecration are only conditions upon which God works?

Yes. It is very important that you clearly understand that it is God who saves and that your consecration and faith are the conditions on which God's saving and sanctifying grace is given.

Reading Club Guide

Which of the conditions seems most difficult to you? Why?

Have you stumbled at the simplicity of faith?

Has this chapter been sufficient for you to get up and move on?

What, if anything, hinders you? How can you defeat this challenge?

---

[1] Some Salvationists actually use Booth's description of "independent" as a term for people who do not depend on Jesus yet. So, "independents" becomes a synonym for sinners, pagans, heathen, pre-Christians, unbelievers, and so on.

[2] Genesis 15:11,17.

PART 1 | Section 20

Sanctification. Objections.

1. You may have noticed that most Christians do not live lives characterized by this blessing. How is this?

They do not know anything about it. It is seldom, or never, preached, or written about in Christian magazines or websites or blogs.[1] Very few people possess the blessing, and, therefore, very few people profess it or talk about it. Consequently, the world is in all but total darkness on the subject.

2. But how is it people don't see holiness in their Bibles, when its pages are splattered with this doctrine?

Because, from their childhood, they have been taught that it is impossible to live without sin; and all the passages teaching the contrary have been explained away—that is, they have been shown to mean something quite different.

3. Don't many zealous Christians strongly oppose this doctrine?

Yes, bitterly so. On no topic do they get more readily positive or angry than when arguing in favor of the continued existence of a little sin in their souls.

4. How do you account for this strong feeling of opposition to so precious and God-honoring a truth?

One reason is that the Christians they know don't experience it and assert that no one else can attain it either.

5. How do you debunk this objection?

What God commands and promises in the Bible is the standard of experience for Christians, not the substandard attainments of His apparent children. Measure yourself by what God says, and not by what His unfaithful followers do.

> "Check their predictions against My testimony," says the LORD. "If their predictions are different from Mine, it is because there is no light or truth in them." *(Isaiah 8:20 NLT)*
>
> Oh, don't worry; I wouldn't dare say that I am as wonderful as these other men who tell you how important they are! But they are only comparing themselves with each other, and measuring themselves by themselves. What foolishness! *(2 Corinthians 10:12 NLT)*

6. What other objection do people bring against this doctrine?

Objectors get it confused with mistaken and proud notions of sinless perfection, and, without stopping to ask or distinguish, they fight against something we also believe is false (sinless perfection—the idea that some people cannot or never even fall short of the glory of God).

7. Are there other objections?

Yes. Others hastily reject it because a few isolated passages of Scripture, ripped out of context, seem to contradict the experience. The main "proof" of objectors is 1 John 1:8,

> If we say we have no sin, we are only fooling ourselves and refusing to accept the truth.

8. But what does John mean when he says, in that passage, "If we say we have no sin, we are only fooling ourselves and refusing to accept the truth"?

You can interpret it two ways, and it can be applied to two different characters:

i. It means that you say, as many do, that you are not a sinner, that you have never done wrong, and have nothing to be forgiven, and therefore, do not need a Savior's blood, well, you deny what every single person knows deep down to be true—namely, that you are, by both nature and practice, a sinner, needing mercy. And, in this denial, you prove that you are fooling yourself and refusing to accept the truth.

ii. This passage also describes and applies to those who, while admitting that they are daily and hourly committing sin, yet delude themselves with the notion that their sins are somehow imputed to Christ, and not charged to them. By this they mean that, no matter how worldly, selfish, or even devilish they may actually be, their sins were so dealt with by

> Christ that they are not imputed to them, and that, therefore, while full of sin, they have no sin.

Actually, this doctrine is known as "perfection in Christ." It states that when God looks at His Children, He looks at them through His Son, and cannot, or does not, or will not see their sins, neither does He take any account of them, nor hold them responsible for them. It asserts that that God looks at them, not as they are, but as they ought to be, and deals with them accordingly. Now, John says in this text, to those who hold these views, "If you say you have no sin, when you are actually committing sin; or if you imagine that when you commit sin, it is not you that does it, but some other nature within you, and that God will not hold you accountable for it; or if in any other way you say you are not a sinner, when you are, you are fooling yourself and refusing to accept the truth."

9. But what is the true meaning of this passage?

We've already stated it—that if you say you are righteous while living in known sin, you deceive yourself. But, if you confess your sins, God is faithful to His own promise of salvation, and just to His Son, who bought it with His blood, to forgive us our sins, and to cleanse us from all unrighteousness.

10. If all of my sins are forgiven, and all my unrighteousness is cleansed away, will there be any left?

No. Certainly not.

11. Then if I am so forgiven and cleansed am I without sin?

Yes, without sin.

12. Can God keep me without sin?

Yes. He has promised to preserve you blameless to the day of His coming as you continue to fulfill the conditions.

13. What other objections are made to this doctrine of holiness?

Objectors say they have never seen a holy person—that is, one who lives without sin.

14. How do you respond to that?

We might suggest:

i. That we are afraid they have not chosen as associates people who believe in the possibility of being holy on earth, and, therefore, they were not likely to meet with many who had attained holiness; and

ii. That we are afraid that, if they had ever met a sanctified person, their beliefs will likely have prevented them recognizing him or her as such. We see the limiting power of beliefs in the case of the Pharisees, who, when they saw the Savior, who, unquestionably, was without sin, still said of Him, "He has a devil."

15. When people say, "Show me a holy person, and then I will believe the doctrine," what do they usually mean?

They are generally influenced by the same feelings as motivated Herod, who searched for the young Child, Jesus, not to believe in Him, but to kill Him. If you presented them with the very character they asked for, their first business would be to pull that person to pieces.

16. Are there any other reasons that seem to account for the ignorance and opposition so prevalent with respect to holiness?

In some cases, it is the result of judicial blindness. That is, God has given them up to their own delusion, that sin is a necessity, and they really believe their own lies. Somewhere back in their history they faced the fact that Jesus saves His people from their sins. They came to the verge of the Canaan land of perfect love and holiness, and because they were not willing to comply with the conditions, and so go up and possess the good land, they were driven back into the wilderness, and given up to perverseness and blindness and unbelief on the subject.

And we're not surprised, seeing how antagonistic holiness doctrines and holy people are to the reign and power of Satan, that Satan hates them, and, so inspires and stirs up as much bitterness and opposition, both to the doctrine and those who profess it, as he can.

17. What is the best advice to give these and all other objectors?

Fully consecrate yourselves to God's service, promising to obey whatever He reveals to you, and you can rest assured that the Holy Spirit will lead you into the truth on the subject.

Reading Club Guide

Do you have any of these objections? Have they been satisfactorily addressed?

Have you any other objections? How do your reading club friends respond to them?

What is the most difficult part of this to believe? Why?

---

[1] Although we invite you to our armybarmy blog, which does talk about it a lot! (http://armybarmyblog.blogspot.ca)

PART 1 | Section 21

Sanctification. The fruits.

1. Are there fruits of holiness by which you can test its presence?

There are fruits by which you can confirm that you have been newly sanctified, although if you've lived a devoted life before attaining it, there may not appear to be a great difference to other people.

2. What are some of these fruits?

i. There is perfect peace in the soul, which is only enjoyed by those in whose souls all controversy with God has ceased.

ii. Generally speaking, there is a great deal of joy, and often periods of heavenly rapture.

iii. A simple, constant trust in God with regard to the expectation of great spiritual wonders and blessings.

iv. A perfect and hearty agreement with the will of God as to all we must do or bear.

v. Great tenderness of heart towards God and people, with watchful eagerness to serve both to the uttermost.

vi. An all-absorbing devotion to the love and service of

God, destroying all love of worldly pleasure and ambition.

vii. A special and complete victory over every sinful harassment, passion, or habit which has been a cause of sin before, and usually perfect deliverance from the harassment itself.

3. Are there any special fruits of Sanctification commonly noticed amongst the Soldiers of The Salvation Army?

Yes, for these people, having been taught previously on certain responsibilities in which they had failed to measure up, are now remarkable for their faithfulness in those matters. For instance,

i. The use of tobacco, drugs, alcohol, and of worldly clothing or ornament is at once given up, as are, also, all worldly companionships or associations.

ii. In the wearing of the Army's uniform or badges, where there has been any hanging back before, here is now the greatest willingness to conform to all Army regulations for Christ's sake.

iii. Those who have been backward in attending or unwilling to speak at the outdoor meetings, or negligent to any other duty, are now not only willing but eager to do all they can.

iv. Those who have before caused trouble by their light and trifling conduct, evil-speaking, jealousy, or unkindness to comrades, are now serious, earnest, humble, and kind to all.

4. Are there any other special fruits of sanctification noticed in the officers of The Salvation Army?

Yes. For it is impossible to be spiritually powerful officer without the enjoyment of this blessing.[1] Almost every officer has, at one time or another, possessed it, too; so that one might think that those who do not possess it must be in a fallen condition, and more or less wretched and untrue.[2] Therefore—

i. Sanctified officers show a real hearty interest in all they do, which is impossible for anyone who is doing what is customary without a whole heart.

ii. They will show a real, careful, earnest love for all their people, without partiality or respect of persons.

iii. They are full of brotherly love to all other officers, esteeming others better than themselves, and willing that others should be honored equally with or more than themselves.

iv. They prefer, in every way, the interests of The Salvation Army to their own ease and advantage, and are, therefore, always to be relied on to carry out orders, or whatever instructions they may receive, without grumbling or hesitation.[3]

v. They are able calmly to trust in God in the midst of difficulties of every kind, restlessly to push on after victory, and humbly to remain child-like amidst the greatest success.

vi. All their life, in private as well as in public, proves that they are really living for God alone, their whole manner tending to draw everyone around them nearer to God and to self sacrifice for Him.

Reading Club Guide

In holy people you know, how is this fruit evident?

Do you have this fruit in your life? How?

Do you agree with the specific Salvationist fruits described? Discuss.

---

[1] Booth's term was "efficient officer." General Eva Burrows suggests that we understand "efficient" as "spiritually powerful" today.

[2] Believe it or not, we've softened Booth's original assertion. It gives one pause to consider the spiritual standards of his Army.

[3] "Comrades, we want more prayer and less pride; more simple faith and less self-sufficiency; more self-denial, less self-pleasing; more faithfulness, less suavity; more regarding The Salvation Army as our Jerusalem and less regard and attention to keeping good friends with Mammon... I have no interest under heaven but what is in The Salvation Army. As a man defends his treasure with all his powers, so will I be true to my pledge to God and to my General, and stand for the principles and doctrine and spirit of the Army with all my might" (Colonel John Dean).

PART 1 | Section 22

Backsliding.

1. What are your views on the subject of backsliding?

We believe it is possible for those who have been truly converted to fall away and be finally lost.

2. How do you prove this?

We all have an inward conviction that if we neglect to watch and pray and obey God in everything, we shall grieve the Spirit of God, and be in danger of falling into sin and making God depart from us.

3. How else do you prove this?

The Bible exhorts the saints to persevere in goodness. In these exhortations God reveals to us that our final salvation depends on our continued obedience and faith, and that if we cease to conform to these conditions we cannot expect Him to continue blessing up with enjoyments of salvation.

> But those who endure to the end will be saved. *(Matthew 24:13 NLT)*
>
> Remember that in a race everyone runs, but only one

> person gets the prize. You also must run in such a way that you will win. *(1 Corinthians 9:24 NLT)*
>
> For if we are faithful to the end, trusting God just as firmly as when we first believed, we will share in all that belongs to Christ. *(Hebrews 3:14 NLT)*
>
> God's promise of entering his place of rest still stands, so we ought to tremble with fear that some of you might fail to get there. *(Hebrews 4:1 NLT)*
>
> Be careful! Watch out for attacks from the devil, your great enemy. He prowls around like a roaring lion, looking for some victim to devour. *(1 Peter 5:8)*
>
> Don't be afraid of what you are about to suffer. The devil will throw some of you into prison and put you to the test. You will be persecuted for ten days. Remain faithful even when facing death, and I will give you the crown of life. *(Revelation 2:10)*

4. Is there any other Scriptural argument proving the possibility of backsliding?

Yes, the warnings of the Bible prove that you can fall away from God after having known His love, and end up in hell. These texts are meaningless and unnecessary if the possibility is contrived and unreal. The emphasis in Scripture suggests that the danger of falling away is huge.

> When righteous people turn from being good and start doing sinful things, they will die for it. Yes, they will die because of their sinful deeds. *(Ezekiel 28:26 NLT)*

> You are the salt of the earth. But what good is salt if it has lost its flavor? Can you make it useful again? It will be thrown out and trampled underfoot as worthless. *(Matthew 5:13 NLT)*

> He cuts off every branch that doesn't produce fruit, and He prunes the branches that do bear fruit so they will produce even more... Anyone who parts from me is thrown away like a useless branch and withers. Such branches are gathered into a pile to be burned. *(John 15:2,6 NLT)*

> Notice how God is both kind and severe. He is severe to those who disobeyed, but kind to you as you continue to trust in his kindness. But if you stop trusting, you also will be cut off. *(Romans 11:22 NLT)*

> Look, I am coming quickly. Hold on to what you have, so that no one will take away your crown. *(Revelation 3:11 NLT)*

5. Is there any other argument?

Yes, the terrible descriptions and examples of apostasy given in the Bible prove the possibility of it. If it had been impossible to so fall from grace as these passages describe, it is simply more than useless to insert them in the Bible.

> Timothy, my son, here are my instructions for you, based on the prophetic words spoken about you earlier. May they give you the confidence to fight well in the Lord's battles. *(1 Timothy 1:18 NLT)*

> They make these proverbs come true: "A dog returns to its vomit," and "A washed pig returns to the mud." *(2 Peter 2:22 NLT)*

We know it is ready because the Scriptures mention the seventh day, saying, "On the seventh day God rested from all his work." But in the other passage God said, "They will never enter my place of rest." So God's rest is there for people to enter. But those who formerly heard the Good News failed to enter because they disobeyed God. *(Hebrews 4:4-6 NLT)*

Dear friends, if we deliberately continue sinning after we have received a full knowledge of the truth, there is no other sacrifice that will cover these sins. There will be nothing to look forward to but the terrible expectation of God's judgment and the raging fire that will consume His enemies. Anyone who refused to obey the law of Moses was put to death without mercy on the testimony of two or three witnesses. Think how much more terrible the punishment will be for those who have trampled on the Son of God and have treated the blood of the covenant as if it were common and unholy. Such people have insulted and enraged the Holy Spirit who brings God's mercy to His people. (Hebrews 10:26-29 NLT).[1]

Reading Club Guide

Have you ever experienced a backslide? Discuss.

What are the ramifications on evangelism of this doctrine?

What safeguards can you put in place to protect against backsliding?

---

[1] Or read the history of Ananias and Sapphira as given in Acts 5:1-11. See also verses such as Proverbs 4:23; Matthew 5:13; John 15:6; Galatians 5:4; Luke 9:62; 8:32; Hebrews 6:4-6; 2 Peter 2:20-22; etc. on backsliding in general. Final salvation is promised to those who endure to the end (see Colossians 1:22,23; Hebrews 3:14; 10:38-39; Jude 20,21; Matthew 10:22; 24:13; Revelation 2:10).

PART 1 | Section 23

Final Perseverance.

1. Don't many people believe much differently than the doctrine of the last section?

Yes. They say that a person once truly saved can never be lost, and they call this doctrine final perseverance.

2. Do they mean by final perseverance that every saint will finally persevere in holiness, and so be finally saved?

Tragically, not! They mean that every saint will be finally saved, whether or not they persevere in holiness. In other words, even if you backslide every now and then, and admit this is all but certain, if you have been truly saved you will certainly be restored in the end, and taken to heaven.

3. On what arguments do they usually rely to support their doctrine?

i. It is said that, at the new birth, another soul, or nature, is born into the regenerated person, which they say is the child of God, and which can never be sent to hell. This view is answered in Section 13.

ii. They support this doctrine by all those texts which speak of the security of faithful saints, such as:

iii. My sheep recognize My voice; I know them, and they follow Me. I give them eternal life, and they will never perish. No one will snatch them away from Me. *(John 10:27-28 NLT)*

4. What is the real meaning of this passage?

It means that Jesus Christ's true disciples know Him, and He knows them, and they follow or are faithful to Him, and that He gives these faithful followers eternal life when this short life is over, and that they shall never perish. The text means the same thing as that which says, "Remain faithful even when facing death, and I will give you the crown of life" (Revelation 2:10 NLT), and this is just what we mean. It cannot, in any way, be made to mean that He gives eternal life to those who don't and won't follow Him, because He says just the opposite to this over and over again. He says He has no pleasure in those who draw back, and that He will spew the lukewarm out of His mouth *(see Revelation 3:16)*.

5. What other text do they quote?

> And all who believe in God's Son have eternal life. *(John 3:36a NLT)*

They argue from this verse that if you believe once, you've guaranteed yourself eternal life, no matter how you live out your years.

6. What is the meaning of this passage?

Two things: First, "All who believe in God's Son have eternal life," really means you who "keep on believing" in the Son, making it clear that if you do not keep on believing[1], you will not keep on having or receiving eternal life. Second, those who use this verse as a pretext ought at least to acknowledge the context of the second half of the verse, which says, "Those who don't obey the Son will never experience eternal life, but the wrath of God remains upon them" *(John 3:36b NLT).*

7. How is it that so many mistakes are made in these and similar passages?

Because people do not observe that the promises of the Bible are made not to particular persons, but to particular characters. For instance, God may agree to give eternal life to those who are His sheep, who are faithful, who persevere, while He condemns, in the plainest and strongest manner, those who cease to be His sheep by proving unfaithful to their trust, and by going back from following Him.

8. How else do they argue in favor of final perseverance?

The argument grounded on the doctrine of election answered in section 8.

Reading Club Guide

How have you addressed this line of reasoning in the past?

How has this chapter strengthened your faith and apologetics on it?

How does this affect your evangelizing?

---

[1] This is the true interpretation of the Greek (see Dean Alford and the Greek scholars).

PART 1 | Section 24

Death and After.

1. What happens to a Salvation Soldier at death?

If faithful to God and the Army, you die as a hero in full triumph, surrounded by your converted family and encouraged comrades, and supported by your glorified Savior.

2. What happens to the Salvation Soldier after death?

Your comrades give you a triumphant funeral, while the story of your holy life and happy death stimulates your comrades to carry on the fight more desperately than before, and leads a number of souls to give themselves to God.

3. But what becomes of the Salvation Soldier's soul?

Your glorified spirit enters Heaven the moment it leaves the body, and is welcomed by God and the angels and the blood-washed Soldiers with whom you fought below. In Heaven, you will probably be employed in some service for the King, for which your military training on earth has specially qualified you.[1]

4. But what becomes of the body after death? Does that live again?

Yes. At the morning of the resurrection, the bodies of the saints are raised and made perfect and re-united with the soul, from which they were separated at death, and then, perfectly redeemed from all the consequences of sin, the glorious service of God is engaged in forever. Even so the bodies of sinners, raised at the same time, and re-united with the spirits that were their companions in sin on the earth, will share the punishment from which they would not allow God to save them.

5. But isn't it difficult to explain how this resurrection can take place?

Yes, very difficult. But any difficulty in either explaining or understanding it does not affect or alter the fact. There is a difficulty in explaining and understanding how a grain of wheat can fall into the earth and die, and live again, and then spring up in beauty and perfection, but there is no denying the fact.

It is the same way for the resurrection of the dead. Our earthly bodies, which die and decay, will be different when they are resurrected, for they will never die. Our bodies now disappoint us, but when they are raised, they will be full of glory. They are weak now, but when they are raised, they will be full of power. They are natural human bodies now, but when they are raised, they will be spiritual bodies. For just as there are natural bodies, so also there are spiritual bodies.

> The Scriptures tell us, "The first man, Adam, became a living person." But the last Adam—that is, Christ—is a life-giving Spirit. *(1 Corinthians 15:42-45 NLT)*

6. What are your views of the Judgment Day?

That in the end of the world there will be a general judgment of all humanity, when the righteous will be acknowledged, vindicated, and rewarded, and the wicked will be discovered and condemned and punished.

7. What does the Army believe on the subject of the Second Coming of Christ?

We believe that in the end of the world, Christ will come again, even as He went away, according to His own words, that is, "in the clouds of heaven, in the glory of His Father, and with all His holy angels."

> It will happen in a moment, in the blinking of an eye, when the last trumpet is blown. For when the trumpet sounds the Christians who have died will be raised with transformed bodies. And then we who are living will be transformed so that we will never die. *(1 Corinthians 15:52 NLT)*

8. But what is the view of the Army on the subject of the Second Coming of Christ to reign personally on the earth?

It does not pretend to determine a subject on which there has been, and is still, so much difference of opinion. But we incline to the opinion that He will not come until the last day of judgment, and rejoice to know that, should He come before then, it will be so much better than our expectation.

9. What are your views about Heaven?

God has somewhere a glorious world to which He intends, in the end, to bring all His faithful soldiers, where they will be holy, useful, and happy forever and ever.

> There are many rooms in My Father's home, and I am going to prepare a place for you. If this were not so, I would tell you plainly. *(John 14:2 NLT)*

Reading Club Guide

How does this chapter build your faith in and anticipation of heaven?

---

[1] Points 3 and 4 in this section deal with a subject about which we speculate to some degree. The answers in the text represent Booth's best take on it at the time. There are other valid perspectives. For those interested, we point you to further research based on the content and references in The Salvation Army Handbook of Doctrine.

PART 1 | Section 25

Hell.

1. Do you believe in Hell?

Yes, all the time.

2. What is Hell?

The place of punishment into which God consigns the wicked after death.

3. Do you believe that this punishment will last forever?

Yes, forever.

4. Are there not some who deny the unending character of this punishment?

Yes. Two different denials are given.

5. What are they?

The first group of people believe that though people are sent to hell at death, or some time after death, and yet that the punishment has such a reforming effect upon them that they get saved in hell, and made fit for heaven, and, in the end, are taken there; so that, at last, the devil and all the lost souls meet with the glorious angels and the blood-washed saints before the throne. This is called the restoration theory.

6. What objections have you to this doctrine?

i. It is in direct opposition to the Bible, which declares, "those who speak against the Son of Man may be forgiven, but anyone who speaks blasphemies against the Holy Spirit will never be forgiven" *(Luke 12:10 NLT)*, or, in an older translation, "it shall not be forgiven him, *neither in this world nor in the world to come*."

Let the one who is doing wrong continue to do wrong; the one who is vile, continue to be vile; the one who is good, continue to do good; and the one who is holy, continue in holiness. *(Revelation 22:11 NLT)*

ii. It makes the torments of hell to be more efficacious in saving and purifying sinners than the blood of Christ and the strivings of the Holy Spirit, and is therefore in direct opposition to the Savior's words, when He said, "If they won't listen to Moses and the prophets, they won't listen even if someone rises from the dead." *(Luke 26:31 NLT)*

7. What is the other view denying the everlasting nature of Hell's punishment?

The other group of objectors says that, after a certain period of punishment, the soul is annihilated—that is, destroyed.

8. Isn't this doctrine false?

Yes, of course.

9. But how can you prove that the punishment of Hell will last forever?

For starters, because all orthodox Christians—that is, those who really believe in the Godhead and Atonement of Jesus Christ—have always believed so, and we do not think that the Holy Spirit, whose business it is to keep the church of God right in doctrine, would have allowed them to be in error all this time on a subject so important.

10. What other argument have you for this doctrine?

Because it is a plain doctrine of the Bible.

> But cowards who turn away from Me, and unbelievers, and the corrupt, and murderers, and the immoral, and those who practice witchcraft, and idol worshipers, and

> all liars—their doom is in the lake that burns with fire and sulfur. This is the second death. *(Revelation 21:8 NLT)*
>
> The smoke of their torment rises forever and ever, and they will have no relief day or night, for they have worshipped the beast and his statue and have accepted the mark of his name. *(Revelation 14:11 NLT)*
>
> Then the devil, who betrayed them, was thrown into the lake of fire that burns with sulfur, joining the beast and the false prophet. There they will be tormented day and night forever and ever. *(Revelation 20:10 NLT)*

These verses explain that unbelievers end up in a lake of fire that torments forever and ever.

> If your hand causes you to sin, cut it off. It is better to enter heaven with only one hand than to go into the unquenchable fires of hell with two hands... And if your eye causes you to sin, gouge it out. It is better to enter the Kingdom of God half blind than to have two eyes and be thrown into hell, "where the worm never dies and the fire never goes out." *(Mark 9:43, 47-48 NLT)*
>
> Then the King will turn to those on the left and say, "Away with you, you cursed ones, into the eternal fire prepared for the devil and his demons!" *(Matthew 25:41 NLT)*
>
> And the list goes on and includes "everlasting destruction" *(2 Thessalonians 1:9)*, "eternal fire that will punish all who are evil" *(Jude 7 NLT)*, "everlasting gloom and darkness" *(Jude 13 NLT)*, "smoke of their torment (rising) forever" *(Revelation 14:11 NLT)*, "everlasting contempt" *(Daniel 12:2)*, and "eternal sin" *(Mark 3:29)*.

11. Are there any other arguments?

Yes. The very same language used by the Holy Spirit to describe the duration of the happiness and joy of the saved is employed to describe the duration of the punishment of the lost.

> And they will go away into eternal punishment, but the righteous will go into eternal life. *(Matthew 25:46 NLT)*[1]

Reading Club Guide

Do you agree with this teaching on Hell? Discuss.

How does this belief affect your relationships with independents (people who don't yet depend on Jesus)?

What should be your attitude towards Christians who disagree with you on this?

---

[1] Other arguments consider such things as: "eternal judgment" being part of "the basics of Christianity" (Revelation 6:2 NLT); the "certain rich man"—a specific person—in the story that includes Lazarus and Abraham (Luke 16:19ff); and the lake of fire hosting torment "day and night forever and ever" (Revelation 20:10).

PART 1 | Section 26

The Bible.

1. What is the meaning of the word Bible?

It means The Book—that is, the Book of books; others are only books, but this is "The Book."

2. Explain what you mean when you say that the Bible is the Word of God.

We mean that God has caused His mind on the subject of our deliverance, duty, and destiny to be written and preserved in this volume, so that this book really contains the statement of His judgment and will concerning humanity, and is, therefore, the Word of God, or the revelation of His mind on the subject. God has put His heart on paper.

3. But how does the Bible reveal the mind of God?

Because —

i. It contains a large number of messages sent directly by God to people, through the medium of the prophets and apostles, and, indirectly, through them to us and all whom they may concern;

ii. The histories, biographies, and facts of the Bible reveal exactly how God feels to people in similar circumstances, and are, therefore, a revelation of the mind of God;

iii. (This is especially true of the life, death, and teaching of Jesus Christ);

iv. The Bible is full of God's thoughts about all the possible conditions of people in time and eternity;

v. It was written directly under the direction or inspiration of God's Spirit.

> You must understand that no prophecy in Scripture ever came from the prophets themselves or because they wanted to prophesy. It was the Holy Spirit who moved the prophets to speak from God. *(2 Peter 1:21. NLT)*

4. In what way did this direction or inspiration enable these people to write the Bible?

The Holy Spirit not only preserved these holy people from mistake, and enabled them to write the exact truth concerning the facts they recorded, but also enabled them to communicate the mind and will of God to us.

5. What evidence have you to show that the Bible is divine, beyond the claim to inspiration of the writers themselves?

The character of the book proves this—

i. The prophecies it contains of events which came to pass

hundreds of years after they were written;

ii. The miracles it records performed by the writers and by others in conjunction with them;

iii. The high morality taught all through it;

iv. The claim made in it of its own inspiration;

v. The revelation it makes of the future;

vi. The style of the book, so different from that of any other;

vii. The influence of the teaching of the book on all individuals and nations who have in any form accepted it;

viii. The book must have been written either by bad or by good people.

Bad people could not have written such a good book, if they would; and they would not have written a book, which so condemned them, here and hereafter, if they could.

Good people would not have written a book which they knew to be false, claiming all the time to be inspired by God.

Accordingly, it must have been written by good people, who were themselves the personal witnesses, in nearly all cases, of the wonderful miracles they record, any one of which is a sufficient and unanswerable argument for the divine origin of the whole.

6. Is the knowledge and belief of the words of the Bible taken alone sufficient for my salvation?

Oh, no, not unless you respond in obedience to Jesus! The Bible is but a means to an end. It is simply God's message to you, telling you and everyone else that if you seek, trust and obey Him you shall be saved, sanctified, and glorified.

7. How am I—a Salvation Army Soldier—to make the best use of my Bible?

i. Read it on your knees;

ii. Read a little at a time;

iii. Read in faith, believing every word you say;

iv. Depend on the Holy Spirit to reveal the real meaning to your soul;

v. Commit the most practical portion to memory;

vi. Explain what you read to the people in words and with illustrations that they can understand.

8. Don't some people set a false value on the Bible?

Yes, some undervalue it, and, in consequence, neglect to read and be governed by its teaching, while others over-estimate it by regarding it as the only way in which God speaks to people.

9. Does God communicate His will to people in any other way than through the written Word?

Yes. He speaks directly to the heart by His Spirit, and by His Spirit also through one person to another.[1]

10. How can you show this?

In two ways—

i. It has been His custom from the beginning to raise up prophets who shall directly convey His wishes to people;

ii. The Savior promised that the Holy Spirit, the Comforter, should be given to His people to lead them into all truth!

   "And I will ask the Father, and He will give you another Counselor, who will never leave you" *(John 14:16. NLT)*.

11. Does this promise apply to us, and may we expect its fulfillment?

Certainly we may. The notion that the fulfillment of this promise was confined to apostolic time is one of the greatest mistakes ever made. It is therefore wrong and misleading to argue that we have no other way of ascertaining the mind of the Spirit concerning our own salvation, or our duty to our fellows, except through the written word. And it is one great cause of so much tame experience in the knowledge of God, and so much lame effort to extend the kingdom of God. The living, active, positive agency of God is comparatively shut out of the world, and a dead book placed in its stead.

12. What authority has the Bible with the Army?

While we hold that God does, by His Spirit, speak as directly to His people in this age as in any other still the Army does solemnly and most emphatically regard the Bible as the divinely authorized standard by which all other professed revelation are to be tested. If this other "revelation" does not line up with the biblical standard, then this revelation is rejected. Whatever is contrary to the teaching of this Book must be considered false, and thrown overboard.

> "Check their predictions against my testimony," says the LORD. "If their predictions are different from Mine, it is because there is no light or truth in them." *(Isaiah 8:20. NLT)*

Reading Club Guide

What authority does the Bible have in your life?
How can you apply point seven?

[1] One approach tests, "is it biblical, Christological, and moral?"

PART 1 | Section 27

Getting People Saved.

1. What is the ordinary condition of Sinners when you meet with them?

Preoccupied. That is—

- Taken up with the things of the world—
- Rebels against God, and—
- Condemned to everlasting punishment.

2. What is your business with them?

i. To secure their attention;

ii. To persuade them to submit to God,[1] and then—

iii. To accept forgiveness through the blood.

3. How do you go about accomplishing this?

By talking to them publicly, in the open-air and indoors, about their own sin, ingratitude, and death; about judgment, hell, and heaven; the love of God and the voluntary suffering and death Jesus Christ endured on their behalf; concerning their influence on others, and other similar topics.

4. What do you do then?

Go among them in the meetings, after the meetings, or wherever you can find them, and converse with them personally—press the truth home—if only a little moved, convict them further. Make them feel, have no pity on them until they are willing to give up all and submit to God.

5. But suppose they are not willing to submit, even if they're convicted and admit that what you are saying is true?

Find out what the hindrance is, and press them to give it up. Show them that it is better to cut off the right hand than to go into hell with two hands, into the fire that never gets quenched.

6. Well, supposing they are willing to give up and be saved, what then?

Test them further by taking them to the mercy seat, and pledge them publicly, and when there, offer them mercy, and pray with and for them.

7. But if they do not get saved, what then?

There is still something in the way. Or it may be, as it frequently is, simply their unbelief, in which case, encourage and instruct and help them. Give them texts and explanations and illustrations and songs, and, above all, a lot of sympathy. Make them pray aloud for themselves. Sing words having faith in them. Make them look at the blood, and trust the loving, dying Christ. Push them into the fountain.

8. If they don't get satisfaction, what must be done next?

Never tell them they are saved, if they don't think so. When you get saved, God will tell you about it, and then you will not need us to tell you so. But encourage them to go on seeking. Urge them to go and deal with God alone, and come again. Get their addresses; have them visited. Go after them yourself.

9. What are you to do next, if they get saved?

Give God all the glory, and get everybody in the place to help you to do it.

10. And what will you do with your convert when you have got her?

Having made them into Saints, now make them into Soldiers. That is, let them—

i. Sign the pledge[2];

ii. Testify at once to the blessing they have found;

iii. Take their name and address for the Army;

iv. Have them at the open-air the next night, with a badge on;

v. Watch over and care for them as if they were your own, and as if you will have to give an account of them at the last day, which you will most certainly have to do.

11. Is it not important that sinners should be intensely serious before they are invited to the penitent-form?

Yes, certainly. It is most disastrous to bring people forward who are not, so far as we can judge, very serious about getting saved.

12. Is it not equally important that the penitents should be properly dealt with when they do come to the mercy seat?

Yes. Let the most experienced people you have deal with them. Speak to them yourself whenever you can. Never be in a hurry, and don't let them go away, if possible, until they are satisfied.

Reading Club Guide

How does this chapter affect your evangelizing?

Who are you currently evangelizing? (Share lists for prayer.)

---

[1] This might involve much discussion, teaching, apologetics, demonstration that God exists, cares, and has the power to intervene in our lives, and prayer. We're looking for people to repent and believe.

[2] We advocate all of these actions, but suggest that the covenanting of soldiership occur, in this era, at the end of the list instead of the front. In some corps today that list is played out with the following conditions:

Been saved for a year.

Been clean for a year.

Completed discipling course and Salvationism 101.

Relationship in a cell.

Relationship in a recognized discipleship connection.

Involvement in a brigade activity.

Read the Bible.

Memorized the doctrines.

Read, internalized, and agreed with the Orders and Regulations and Handbook of Doctrine.

Proven a consistent tither.

Agreed to life-long covenant a soldier in The Salvation Army.

Agreed to wear uniform.

PART 1 I Section 28

Women's Right to Preach.[1]

1. When you use women preachers are you acting against the clear teaching of Scripture?

Definitely not. It is true that there is one passage in Paul's writings which at first seems to favor such prohibition, namely:

> Women should be silent during the church meetings. It is not proper for them to speak. They should be submissive, just as the law says. If they have any questions to ask, let them ask their husbands at home, for it is improper for women to speak in church meetings. *(1 Corinthians 14:34-35. NLT)*

But, rightly understood, this passage simply means that Paul thought it a shame for a woman to take any part in the debates which were common in Jewish assemblies at that time, and also in the early churches *(see Acts 28:4-6; Acts 27:1,4,17; Acts 15:5-7)*, and which are not uncommon now in meetings where the claims of Jesus Christ to be the Messiah are discussed. He thought it better that, rather than she should ask any questions there[2], or take any part in these unseemly debates, she would ask her husband for the desired information at home, but the Holy Spirit never intended the Apostle in this passage, or in any other, to prohibit preaching and testifying for Christ.

i. Seeing that in the eleventh chapter of the same epistle, the Apostle lays down the exact dress regulation for women when they do preach;

ii. That under the Old Dispensation some of the most eminent preachers and leaders of His people were women. They were allowed to be even Generals then *(see Judges 4:4,10,11; 2 Kings 22:14-20)*;

iii. That the first officers He commissioned to carry the message of His resurrection were women—

"And as they went, Jesus met them. 'Greetings!' He said. And they ran to Him, held His feet, and worshipped Him. Then Jesus said to them, 'Don't be afraid! Go tell My brothers to leave for Galilee, and they will see Me there'" *(Matthew 28:9-10 NLT)*;

iv. That the same baptism of the Holy Spirit on the day of Pentecost was given to women, and the Apostle Peter confirmed their Divine right to preach by quoting the prophecies of Joel respecting them—

"No, what you see this morning was predicted centuries ago by the prophet Joel... In those days I will pour out my Spirit upon all My servants, men and women alike, and they will prophesy" *(Acts 2:16,18 NLT)*;

v. That they were female "helpers," "yokefellows," "laborers," with the Apostles in the early churches, who preached the Gospel *(see Philippians 4:3, Romans 16:3;14:12);*

vi. Philip, the evangelist, had four daughters, virgins, who prophesied —

"Then we went on to Caesarea and stayed at the home of Philip the Evangelist, one of the seven men who had been chosen to distribute food. He had four unmarried daughters who had the gift of prophecy" *(Acts 21:8-9. NLT);*

vii. Multitudes of women since then, in all lands, have been commissioned by the Holy Spirit to preach the Gospel and lead His people, which commission they have discharged with overwhelming success;

viii. The Holy Spirit in Galatians 3:28 states that there is neither male nor female, but that all are one in Christ Jesus, thereby affirming that, in the privileges, duties, and responsibilities of Christ's Kingdom, all differences on account of sex are abolished—

"There is no longer Jew or Gentile, slave or free, male or female. For you are all Christians – you are one in Christ Jesus" *(Galatians 3:28, NLT).*[3]

Reading Club Guide

Is this an issue for you? Why?

Does this chapter solve any lingering problems?
How can we, in our corps, promote this truth in our daily and weekly warfare?

---

[1] This fits in the doctrine section for two reasons: 1. It is part of Booth's original text, "Doctrines of The Salvation Army," and, 2. It is important teaching for Salvationists.

[2] N.T. Wright demonstrates that the current issue in the Middle East, in which women, in some cases sitting separate from men in the church services, are often at a loss because they are fluent in local dialect but not the classical Arabic used from the pulpit and left to guess and the message conveyed or "grow bored and talk among themselves," is not unlike the situation Paul addresses in this instance (N.T. Wright, "The Biblical Basis for Women's Service in the Church," Priscilla Papers, Volume 20, Number 4, Autumn 2006. p5).

[3] There is much more on this important warfare topic. The argument is full of definitions of "helpmeet" and "head" and "servant" and examples of leaders, generals, apostles, prophets, and preachers. We highly recommend reading Catherine Booth's famous pamphlet, "Female Ministry: Women's Right To Preach The Gospel" (http://www.indiana.edu/~letrs/vwwp/booth/ministry.html). This provides the foundational Salvation Army position on which to base our warfare. But there is even more. Try Danielle Strickland's "The Liberating Truth" (2011), or "Women in the War," issue 44 of Journal of Aggressive Christianity, edited by JoAnn Shade (www.armybarmy.com/pdf/JAC_Issue_044.pdf). See Richard Munn's clarifying study, "Men, Women, and the Bible" in issue 43 of Journal of Aggressive Christianity (www.armybarmy.com/pdf/JAC_Issue_043.pdf). Or read Danielle Strickland's incendiary "Married Woman's Ghetto Rant" in issue 41 of Journal of Aggressive Christianity (www.armybarmy.com/pdf/JAC_Issue_041.pdf). Christians for Biblical Equality also provides a solid resource at www.cbeinternational.org.

PART 1 | Section 29

The Government of the Army.[1]

1. What is the system of Government in the Army?

It most nearly resembles a military system. Without any intention of imitation on the part of its leaders, in the first instance, the Army government has come to be like that form of human government which has been proved to be best adapted for preserving order and making aggression. It is an Army, and therefore it is governed as an Army. This corporate Christian life enjoys many metaphors. In the New Testament, the Church[2] is described as the following: the flock of which Jesus is the Shepherd[3], the Body of Christ of which Jesus is the head[4], a temple or building of which Jesus is the cornerstone[5], a kingdom which is also a family in which Jesus is King[6], the bride of Christ, for whom Jesus is the bridegroom[7]. During this season of history God seems to be emphasizing something more than a metaphor—the Army of God.[8] As Australian Salvationist Anthony Castle asserts, "If we are a metaphorical army in a metaphorical war, then we are not really an army and this is not a war."[9]

2. Does our government offer real freedom to all our people?

Yes, the Army form of government is compatible with the largest amount of personal freedom in combination with the greatest measure of strength. There is in the Army the fullest liberty to be good and to do good. No religious organization ever existed on the face of the earth which combined to so large an extent the two qualities of strength and freedom.

3. Does this enable the best of our people to share in the government?

Yes, most certainly. The government of the Army gives the most absolute certainty that the best and most capable soldiers will have the fullest opportunities of reaching the highest positions of usefulness and power. To rise in the Army, a soldier or an officer has only to prove himself or herself proportionately good and capable.[10] It is really the administration of government by the wisest and best.

4. But has God given any positive direction as to the form of government for His people?

No. The New Testament does not lay down any precise pattern for the government of the Kingdom of Jesus Christ on the earth. Some people say that it does, but they disagree among themselves as to what it is—one denomination argue for one thing, and another for something else.[11]

5. But didn't the Apostles and Early Christians all adopt one plan?

No, and, even if they did, it would still be very difficult to prove that, because they followed certain customs, we are in any way under God's commands to do what they did.

6. How, then, has the Army been guided?

The Army has been guided by the Bible. For, though a model government was not originated by God, and made binding upon His people through all following ages, He has caused certain great principles to be plainly described in the Bible, as fundamental to every form of government which has His approbation, and the government of the Army is in perfect harmony with these principles.[12]

7. Has there been in the past any government similar to ours which has had the approval of God?

Yes, the government of the Army actually presents in its main features a strong resemblance to the government of the Jewish church and nation, which we know were originated and approved by God Himself.

8. Are there any advantages in the Army form of government?

Yes, many. Among others:

i. It is simple. Everybody understands it. No matter how ignorant people may be on other questions, they can understand the way in which an army is governed.

ii. It is powerful. If several persons wish to do a particular work they must pull together, and it is impossible for them to pull together unless they have rules of action to guide them and certain leaders to obey. In the Army, the best methods for doing the work of God are discovered and printed, and are called Orders and Regulations, and the officers and soldiers obey them and fight for God under their command.

iii. It secures unity and harmony. Where measure and methods are discussed and debated by those who have to carry them out, the result is always delay and often disagreement, and therefore often weakness and defeat.

9. Is there any authority in the Bible for this army form of government?

i. Yes, this government of The Salvation Army is fashioned after God's own plan for governing people, as revealed in the Bible.

ii. It is like the plans which God used for the Israelites at different times. For instance, Moses was the General of God's Army in his day: and, later, David and Solomon ruled in much the same way. The government of the early Christian Churches was nearly the same, for it is very probable that Paul was, in fact, if not in name, the General of The Salvation Army of his time, exercising a very similar authority over the churches or societies established by him to that exercised by the head of The Salvation Army now.[13]

Reading Club Guide

What are the advantages of our command structure?

What are safeguards against the enemy's counter-attack to stimulate abuse of the system?

How can we pray for those God has placed in leadership before us?

---

[1] This section is included in part 1, The Doctrines, because is included by Booth in the original book.

[2] Greek: "Ekklesia"—assembly, "that which is called out."

[3] John 10:16.

[4] Romans 12:5.

[5] 1 Peter 2:4,5.

[6] Colossians 1:12,13.

[7] Ephesians 5:25-32.

[8] 1 Chronicles 12:22.

[9] Anthony Castle. 2006. "Are We a Metaphor?" in Journal of Aggressive Christianity, #42.

[10] In the generations since General Booth's promotion to Glory, the remaining questions on this point seem to be soldiers who are not officers and officers who are married women. Neither group seems to fully experience what General Booth has described.

[11] Historically, there are three basic forms of church government: Congregational, Presbyterian, and Episcopal. Congregational is independent of higher authority, with decisions being made by the congregation. Presbyterian model is government by an assembly of elders of the congregation. And Episcopal model is government by the bishops. This latter form recognizes spiritual authority and accountability beyond the local level. Commissioner Phil Needham spun it this way: "The Salvation Army opted for an Episcopal form of government expressed in the language of the military" (Community in Mission, p. 50). A good case could be made that the Army model is more Apostolic than Episcopal.

[12] See point 9.

[13] Suggestion has been made that this book should explain The Salvation Army's position on sacraments. Other books have tackled this subject effectively, from The Salvationist and The Sacraments all the way through to Who Are These Salvationists? But here is another take (the first section is by Lieutenant-Colonel Eugene Pigford, USE Territory):

The word Sacrament is of Latin derivation and has to do with the concept of oath. A Roman Soldier being sworn in to military service would declare the 'Sacramentum', thus swearing his allegiance to his government and his role. In the history of the Church, it has come to mean certain specific religious exercises, through which special blessing or spiritual edification is dispensed. It has been the subject of much debate whether or not these observances are efficacious in and of themselves, or whether they become the associated vehicle through which special blessing is channeled and dispensed, along with but separate from their practice.

And, if the latter is true, are they really necessary? What is the nature and evolution of sacred symbols in scripture?

A. Circumcision

When the Lord reveals Himself to Abram as El-Shaddai and his name is changed to Abraham, the practice of circumcision is introduced with the following direction:

> Then God said to Abraham, "As for you, you must keep My covenant, you and your descendants after you for the generations to come. This is my covenant with you and your descendants after you, the covenant you are to keep. Every male among you shall be circumcised. You are to undergo circumcision and it will be the sign of the covenant between Me and you. For the generations to come every male among you who is 8 days old must be circumcised including those born in your household or bought with money from a foreigner—those who are not your offspring. Whether born in your household or bought with your money they must be circumcised. My covenant in your flesh is to be an everlasting covenant." (Genesis 17:9-13)

In the Old Testament, circumcision was periodically reinforced. Moses was required to circumcise his sons before going to Pharaoh in Egypt (Exodus 4:24). The Israelites circumcised all their males immediately upon crossing the Jordan and prior to taking possession of the Promised Land (Joshua 5).

During the establishment of the early church, there was a contingent seeking to make circumcision a prerequisite for new believers. Paul confronted this error in his letter to the Church at Galatia, "Mark my words, I Paul tell you that if you let yourself be circumcised, Christ will be of no value to you at all .... For in

Christ Jesus neither circumcision nor uncircumcision has any value. The only thing that counts is faith expressing itself through love." (Galatians 5:2,6)

While the rite of circumcision was not practiced by Gentile believers, the term was applied to them in a spiritual context as may be noted in Colossians 2:11, Romans 2:29 and Philippians 3:3. Thus, the importance of the meaning of the practice became a priority over the practice itself.

B. Devoted Things

Periodically, in scripture, the instruction was given to the Israelites that every living thing in a conquered city was to be utterly destroyed and absolutely none of the spoils were to be kept (Joshua 6:21).

The Israelites loss of the battle of Ai and King Saul's loss of his monarchy were both related to disobedience concerning this issue. Samuel the prophet declares, "Does the Lord delight in burnt offerings and sacrifices as much as in obeying the voice of the Lord. To obey is better than sacrifice and to heed is better than the fat of rams" (1 Samuel 15:22).

The apostle Paul is perhaps building on this concept when he declares,

> But whatever was to my profit, I now consider loss for the sake of Christ. What is more, I consider everything a loss compared to the surpassing greatness of knowing Christ Jesus my Lord, for whose sake I have suffered the loss of all things. I consider them rubbish, that I may gain Christ and be found in Him. (Philippians 3:7-8)

Once again the spiritual truth takes precedence over the earlier physical act.

C. The Brazen Serpent

During the wilderness wanderings of the Israelites, they periodically engaged in grumbling and complaining. Numbers 21:6 describes how God sent venomous snakes in judgement upon them and, when they confessed their sin and requested forgiveness and healing God made a provision for them. A bronze serpent was made and fastened to a pole. Anyone who was bitten would be healed if he would look at the bronze snake. 2 Kings 18:4 reveals that this bronze serpent eventually became the object of idolatrous worship and had to be destroyed by King Hezekiah as part of his spiritual reforms. Jesus, in His discourse with Nicodemus uses the analogy of the serpent in the wilderness to describe the necessary death of the Son of Man.

The spiritual lesson and analogy of the wilderness serpent continue to be important. The physical representation of the serpent itself has long since been destroyed.

D. The Ark of the Covenant

This was the most sacred object of all the tabernacle furnishings. It was a wooden box overlaid with gold. Inside of it was a pot of manna, Aaron's rod that budded, and the tablets of stone received by Moses on Mt Sinai. It occupied the central place in the Holy of Holies. It was carried at the head of the procession when the children of Israel were on the move. There were specific instructions for the covering and transporting of the Ark. Any carelessness with regard to these instructions was usually fatal to the transgressor.

The Lord had instructed Moses that He would focus His Presence between the cherubim on the Mercy Seat or the lid of the Ark. We might logically assume that with the specific instruction and severe penalties associated with proper regard for the Ark, that it would have a place of permanence in the worship setting of the Israelites. However, after the destruction of Jerusalem in 586 B.C. Jeremiah prophesies that, "Men will no longer say, 'The Ark of the Covenant of the Lord.' It will never enter their minds or be remembered, it will not be missed, nor will another one be made" (Jeremiah 3:16).

From the beginning of the Babylonian captivity, the children of Israel had no access to a temple, tabernacle, or any worship setting that would have had any of their religious symbols. It was during the Captivity that synagogues developed, not as places with the religious symbols that had been so characteristic of the Hebrew faith, but as meeting places where the scriptures could be read, studied, and expounded.

The period of the Captivity was a difficult time for the children of Israel but a time of learning and spiritual discovery as well.

Though they could not encounter Yahweh through their historic religious observances, including Passover, they did discover His overruling hand on their circumstances.

The New Testament introduces radical change to the theological assumptions of the Jewish culture of the day. Although the springboard for the Christian faith is very Jewish in its character, the essential spiritual nature of the Kingdom of God is prominent throughout the gospel writings and the epistles.

At the onset of His ministry, Jesus emphasizes to Nicodemus (John 3) that the transforming experience of conversion is best likened to a spiritual birth. "That which is born of the flesh is flesh, and that which is born of the Spirit is spirit." Similarly, He says to the Samaritan woman, "A time is coming and now has come when the true worshippers will worship the Father in spirit and truth, for they are the kind of worshipers the Father seeks. God is spirit, and His worshipers must worship in spirit and truth" (John 4:23-24).

Jesus on How God Communicates

In fact, some of the Jewish rites themselves become teaching models utilized by Jesus in interpreting the deeper spiritual truths of the Kingdom to the new followers of faith in Him. This is certainly true of the rite of baptism and observance of Passover along with several other Jewish festivals. While intermittent practices of these rites or some modification of them continues into the early church, it should be noted that their continued practice was not without difficulty as may be noted with regard to baptism in 1 Corinthians 1:13-17 and communion in 1 Corinthians 11:17-33.

References to the word "baptize" in Jewish usage appear several times in the Mosaic laws of purification (Exodus 33:17-21; Leviticus 11:23, 15:8; 17:15; Numbers 19:17,18; 31:22,23). Its meaning is that of "washing" or "cleansing" in these instances. In the Septuagint the word is used three times: 2 Kings 5:14, Ecclesiastes 34:25 and Isaiah 21:4. In all of these references the most likely meaning is one of cleansing. John the Baptist introduces a new ethical dimension to the practice by associating it with the necessity for personal repentance. It became a public declaration of a personal decision to change one practices and manner of thinking in preparation for the coming of the Kingdom. In and of itself it is an incomplete act as may be noted in Acts 18:25 and 19:3-5.

But Jesus, Himself, affirms the new emphasis on repentance John has brought to this Jewish rite by Himself participating in the baptism of John. The participation of Jesus in the baptismal event can be most easily understood as the Son of Man, as Jesus often referred to Himself, anticipates the day when He will become the Sinbearer while simultaneously endorsing the preparatory process of John's ministry in announcing Christ's kingdom. In the Septuagint, the Greek word "baptismos" is used to refer to the Jewish rites of the act of washing itself. In the New Testament the word used is "baptisma" which, "always incorporates into its meaning the entire scope of the redemptive significance of the incarnate presence of Christ" (Dr. Clarence Bass).

In the New Testament, the same word is used in an entirely spiritual context. For example, Jesus, subsequent to His baptism by John, says, "I have a baptism to be baptized with" (Luke 12:59), and "Can you drink of the cup that I drink of and be baptized with the baptism that I am baptized with?" (Mark 10:38; Matthew 20:22).

The New Testament makes a strong contrast between John's water baptism and the subsequent baptism of the Holy Spirit. Passages such as Mark 1:8; Matthew 3:11; Luke 3:16; Acts 1:4; and 11:16 all show this emphasis. Throughout the epistles there is growing emphasis on the redemptive, transformative and empowering dimensions of spiritual baptism (e.g. Romans 6:3-5).

Finally, Scripture emphasizes the essentials of faith including the dimensions of "one baptism" Ephesians 4:5 which we would understand to be the essential baptism of the Holy Spirit. (This ends the note by Lt. Colonel Eugene Pigford.)

And, Water Baptism…

The "command" to water baptize:

> Therefore go and make disciples of all nations, baptising them in the name of the Father and of the Son and of the Holy Spirit, and teaching them to obey everything I have commanded you. And surely I am with you always, to the very end of the age. (Matthew 28:19-20)

Peter replied, "Repent and be baptised, every one of you, in the name of Jesus Christ for the forgiveness of your sins. And you will receive the gift of the Holy Spirit" (Acts 2:38).

That sounds convincing (though a case can be made that the Matthew 28 reference does not refer to water). However, we need consider these verses in light of other Scripture. Two parallel texts speak to this issue:

"I baptise you with water for repentance. But after me will come one who is more powerful than I, whose sandals I am not fit to carry. He will baptize you with the Holy Spirit and with fire" (Matthew 3:11).

"For John baptized with water, but in a few days you will be baptized with the Holy Spirit" (Acts 1:5). "But" makes the water obsolete. Just because it was practiced in the New Testament doesn't mean it was a command of God.

The purpose of baptism was to publicly announce that the individual was identifying with the Christians. It also nicely symbolized the death and resurrection experienced by a believer in Christ at conversion. That's it. And the resurrection part was purely a happy coincidence (or a neat addition by God!), since water baptism is not even originally a Christian ritual. Luke's Acts text (2:38) is not a theological treatise. You can't nail theology and practice based on Acts since there are so many different methods used in Acts (if you do, you could as easily assert that the gift of tongues always accompanies the arrival of the Holy Spirit, that martyrdom is the approved church growth method, and communism is the official means of church life...). Theology is not Luke's purpose. In this text Peter commands that they repent and be baptised because the Jews in the crowd needed to associate with the Christians.

If that's the purpose, then there's no reason to continue that today because best-case scenario you'll only get your family and some friends to watch you get dunked. They are the only ones for whom you'll associate with Christians through baptism. Christian t-shirts worn in busy public settings do a much better job of associating with Christians as many more people will see you.

Paul didn't come to do it and yet he was the biggest evangelist ever. Matthew 28 includes two actual commands: go and make disciples. The rest is descriptive.

Jesus was all about the Kingdom. He came to proclaim the arrival of the Kingdom. He sent the disciples to do the same. Nowhere in the descriptions of His commands concerning either His own or His disciples' efforts to establish the Kingdom is there any reference to baptism. Why does the single most important subject in the whole Bible, which deals with turning sinners into saints, not include this water baptism?

The "command" to take communion.

"And He took bread, gave thanks and broke it, and gave it to them, saying, 'This is My body given for you; do this in remembrance of Me'" (Luke 22:19).

That's a pretty spotty command. Remember the context. They were celebrating the Passover supper. There was an elaborate ritual surrounding it, pointing back to the commands of God to the people of Israel to avoid suffering from the last plague on Egypt (Exodus 12). So, in the context of that initial evening, Jesus' instruction for us is that whenever we eat Passover bread and wine we should do it remembering that Jesus is our Passover Lamb! It's an excellent illustration. However, I celebrate the Passover, at most, once a year. How about you? It is an annual holy day.

In the Luke text, Jesus tells the disciples to do this in remembrance. Does that mean that they are supposed to take bread, give thanks, and break it (like Jesus just did)? That is the simple meaning of the text. That's what they did. There is nothing ritualistic in that text.

The Other Account of the Last Supper:

> When He had finished washing their feet, He put on His clothes and returned to His place. "Do you understand what I have done for you?" He asked them. "You call Me 'Teacher'

> and 'Lord,' and rightly so, for that is what I am. Now that I, your Lord and Teacher, have washed your feet, you also should wash one another's feet. I have set you an example that you should do as I have done for you. I tell you the truth, no servant is greater than his master, nor is a messenger greater than the one who sent him. Now that you know these things, you will be blessed if you do them. (John 13:12-17)

At the same last supper, Jesus washes their feet, asks if they understand, asserts that this is an example for them, "you also should wash one another's feet. I have set an example that you should do as I have done for you.... You will be blessed if you do them."

If anything comes out of the last supper, it is definitely foot washing.

Here Jesus projects the actions of a private supper into the future, casting them as an example which, when followed, will bring blessing. If there is anything we are to imitate from this last supper, it is to wash each other's feet.

Why not sacraments in the first place?

Practical

Actually, The Salvation Army practiced sacraments in the first place. The initial reasons for stopping included such practical considerations as;

1) perceived difficulty through the Church with women administering them,

2) having converted drunks drinking alcohol at the Holiness meeting .... Such practicalities are no longer valid hindrances to sacramental practice.

Philosophical

There are good philosophical reasons following close behind. The Salvation Army determined to go ritual-free. This serves as a testimony to the rest of the Body of Christ. There are many people in the Army who are for sacraments, but they have made personal sacrifice to maintain the Army's non-sacramental testimony to the Body.

As one Body (the universal church), the Body still practices the sacraments. Within the Body, the tiny part called The Salvation Army is a living, breathing reminder to the rest of the Body that the sacraments are helps at best, and that, in and of themselves, they don't necessarily convey any blessing that is not available without them. The testimony continues outside of the Body. Whereas much of the Body finds itself in the priestly tradition, into which the rituals of sacraments fit smoothly (priests administer these sacraments, etc.), The Salvation Army has determined to fit into the prophetic tradition.

The prophetic tradition speaks out to society of sin, of God's love, and of the way from one to the other. The focus is on the prophetic, not the priestly. Fittingly (although admittedly not necessarily) we have stripped off some/all of the priestly trimmings from our praxis.

PART 2

Introduction.

1. What role does covenant have in effective soldiership?

Covenant is the much-overlooked key to effective soldiership. Long known as the Soldier's Pledge, the Articles of War have more recently been renamed *A Soldier's Covenant*. And, yet, most Salvationists don't understand the profundity and potential of this rich, Biblical truth. It might persuasively be argued that a universal embrace of covenant is the one means by which The Salvation Army might both position and posture ourselves and mobilize and deploy in the world so that Catherine Booth's prophecy might be something more than bandwagon- wishful thinking:

> The decree has gone forth that the kingdoms of this world shall become the kingdom of our Lord and of His Christ, and that He shall reign, whose right it is, from the River to the ends of the earth. We shall win. It is only a matter of time. I believe that this Movement shall inaugurate the final conquest of our Lord Jesus Christ.

This is truly a revolutionary war cry. And our covenant is crucial to the victory.

2. But isn't covenant legalistic?

If it is, then our God is a legalist God. He is big on covenant.

3. Doesn't Ecclesiastes command us not to make covenant?

That isn't exactly how the passage goes:

> And don't make rash promises to God, for He is in heaven, and you are only here on earth. So let your words be few. Just as being too busy gives you nightmares, being a fool makes you a blabbermouth. So when you make a promise to God, don't delay in following through, for God takes no pleasure in fools. Keep all the promises you make to Him. It is better to say nothing than to promise something that you don't follow through on. *(Ecclesiastes 5:2-5)*

Some use this verse and similar ones in the New Testament to argue that we shouldn't covenant. But that isn't at all what Ecclesiastes is saying. It makes two points:

a. Don't make rash promises to God.
b. It is better to say nothing than to make a promise you don't fulfill.

4. Some have made rash promises of soldiership. What about them?

Some of you have made rash promises in your soldiership covenant. It would have been better for you to say nothing. My friend never became a soldier as a mid-teenager, partly because all of his friends did. That is, they jumped into uniform so that they could go on the next band trip and made rash promises that many of them have broken. My friend followed the biblical advice here and said nothing.

Look how this speaks to the two points:

a. So, we agree that we shouldn't make rash promises. But this says nothing at all about a reasoned, prayed-up, determined covenant of soldiership for life with God through The Salvation Army.

b. But that doesn't make my friend a hero (although he is a good guy!). It just makes some of his friends "blabbermouths" and "fools" (according to the Ecclesiastes five text above).

While it is better to say nothing than to rashly promise, it is even better to make a godly promise and fulfill it. I mean, spectators and television watchers say nothing on record. There is nothing noble in that silence.

5. What is the attraction of covenant?

Of course, it takes guts and conviction to promise. That's part of the attraction. We're not called to some lame membership in a grocery store or the public library, to which we can belong if we're breathing. We're called to something romantically heroic, something that may likely cost us our lives (as it has cost some of our valiant, fallen comrades).

The difference in cost leads to a difference in effect. Your public library and grocery membership card will help you accomplish very little in life. But your covenant with God as a soldier can help you accomplish world conquest (and for you doubters, it can still help you get heaps of people saved who are currently going to hell and end generations of demon-captives).

Reading Club Guide

How is a Soldier's Covenant similar to other covenants people make?

What are the safeguards against covenant becoming legalistic?

Have you embraced your covenant? How might you?

This is the current Articles of War for Salvation Army Soldiers:

Soldier's Covenant

Having accepted Jesus Christ as my Savior and Lord, and desiring to fulfill my membership of His Church on earth as a soldier of The Salvation Army, I now by God's grace enter into a sacred covenant.

I believe and will live by the truths of the word of God expressed in The Salvation Army's eleven articles of faith:

We believe that the Scriptures of the Old and New Testaments were given by inspiration of God; and that they only constitute the Divine rule of Christian faith and practice.

We believe that there is only one God, who is infinitely perfect, the Creator, Preserver, and Governor of all things, and who is the only proper object of religious worship.

We believe that there are three persons in the Godhead—the Father, the Son and the Holy Ghost—undivided in essence and co-equal in power and glory.

We believe that in the person of Jesus Christ the Divine and human natures are united, so that He is truly and properly God and truly and properly man.

We believe that our first parents were created in a state of innocency, but by their disobedience they lost their purity and happiness; and that in consequence of their fall all men have become sinners, totally depraved, and as such are justly exposed to the wrath of God.

We believe that the Lord Jesus Christ has, by His suffering and death, made an atonement for the whole world so that whosoever will may be saved.

We believe that repentance towards God, faith in our Lord Jesus Christ and regeneration by the Holy Spirit are necessary to salvation.

We believe that we are justified by grace, through faith in our Lord Jesus Christ; and that he that believeth hath the witness in himself.

We believe that continuance in a state of salvation depends upon continued obedient faith in Christ.

We believe that it is the privilege of all believers to be wholly sanctified, and that their whole spirit and soul and body may be preserved blameless unto the coming of our Lord Jesus Christ.

We believe in the immortality of the soul; in the resurrection of the body; in the general judgment at the end of the world; in the eternal happiness of the righteous; and in the endless punishment of the wicked.

I will be responsive to the Holy Spirit's work and obedient to His leading in my life, growing in grace through worship, prayer, service and the reading of the Bible. I will make the values of the Kingdom of God and not the values of the world the standard for my life.

I will uphold Christian integrity in every area of my life, allowing nothing in thought, word or deed that is unworthy, unclean, untrue, profane, dishonest or immoral.

I will maintain Christian ideals in all my relationships with others; my family and neighbors, my colleagues and fellow Salvationists, those to whom and for whom I am responsible, and the wider community.

I will uphold the sanctity of marriage and of family life. I will be a faithful steward of my time and gifts, my money and possessions, my body, my mind and my spirit, knowing that I am accountable to God.

I will abstain from alcoholic drink, tobacco, the non-medical use of addictive drugs, gambling, pornography, the occult and all else that could enslave the body or spirit.

I will be faithful to the purposes for which God raised up The Salvation Army, sharing the good news of Jesus Christ, endeavoring to win others to Him, and in His name caring for the needy and the disadvantaged.

I will be actively involved, as I am able, in the life, work, worship and witness of the corps, giving as large a proportion of my income as possible to support its ministries and the worldwide work of the Army.

I will be true to the principles and practices of The Salvation Army, loyal to its leaders, and I will show the spirit of Salvationism whether in times of popularity or persecution.

I now call upon all present to witness that I enter into this covenant and sign these Articles of War of my own free will, convinced that the love of Christ, who died and now lives to save me, requires from me this devotion of my life to His service for the salvation of the whole world; and therefore do here declare my full determination, by God's help, to be a true soldier of The Salvation Army.

Previous Articles of War declarations

Therefore, I do here and now, and forever, renounce the world with all its sinful pleasures, companionships, treasures, and objects, and declare my full determination boldly to show myself a soldier of Jesus Christ in all places and companies, no matter what I may have to suffer, do or lose by so doing.[1]

I do here and now declare that I will abstain from the use of all intoxicating liquor, and from the use of all baneful drugs, except when such drugs shall be ordered for me by a doctor.[2]

I do here and now declare that I will abstain from the use of all low or profane language and from all impurity, including unclean conversation, the reading of any obscene book or paper at any time, in any company, or in any place.[3]

I do here declare that I will not allow myself in any deceit or dishonesty; nor will I practice any fraudulent conduct in my business, my home or in any other relation in which I may stand to my fellow men; but that I will deal truthfully, honorably and kindly with all those who employ me or whom I may myself employ.[4]

I do here declare that I will never treat any woman, child or other person, whose life, comfort or happiness may be placed within my power, in an oppressive, cruel or cowardly manner; but that I will protect such from evil and danger so far as I can, and promote, to the utmost of my ability, their present welfare and eternal Salvation.[5]

I do here declare that I will spend all the time, strength, money and influence I can in supporting and carrying on the Salvation war, and that I will endeavor to lead my family, friends, neighbors and all others whom I can influence to do the same, believing that the sure and only way to remedy all the evils in the world is by bringing men to submit themselves to the government of the Lord Jesus Christ.[6]

I do here declare that I will always obey the lawful orders of my officers, and that I will carry out to the utmost of my power all the orders and regulations of the Army; and, further, that I will be an example of faithfulness to its principles, advance to the utmost of my ability its operations, and never allow, where I can prevent it, any injury to its interest, or hindrance to its success.[7]

And I do here and now call upon all present to witness that I have entered into this undertaking and sign these Articles of War of my own free will, feeling that the love of Christ, who died to save me, requires from me this devotion of my life to His service for the Salvation of the whole world, and therefore do here declare my full determination, by God's help, to be a true soldier of The Salvation Army till I die.[8]

---

[1] The 1890 version, current for General Booth when writing, reads: Therefore, I do here, and now, and for ever, renounce the world with all its sinful pleasures, companionship treasures, and objects, and declare my full determination boldly to show myself a Soldier of Jesus Christ in all places and companies, no matter what I may have to suffer, do, or lose, by so doing.

[2] The 1890 version, current for General Booth when writing, reads: I do here and now declare that I will abstain from the use of all intoxicating liquors, and also from the habitual use of opium, ludanum, morphia, and all other baneful drugs, except when in illness such drugs shall be ordered for me by a doctor.

[3] The 1890 version, current for General Booth, when writing, reads: I do here and now declare that I will abstain from the use of all low or profane language; from the taking of the name of God in vain; and from all impurity, or from taking part in any unclean conversation or the reading of any obscene book or paper at any time, in any company, or in any place.

[4] The 1890 version, current for General Booth, when writing, reads: I do here declare that I will not allow myself in any falsehood, deceit, misrepresentation, or dishonesty; neither will I practice any fraudulent conduct, either in my business, my home, or in any other relation in which I may stand to my fellow men, but that I will deal truthfully, fairly, honorably, and kindly with all those who may employ me or whom I may myself employ.

[5] The 1890 version, current for General Booth, when writing, reads: I do here declare that I will never treat any woman, child, or other person, whose life, comfort, or happiness may be placed within my power, in an oppressive, cruel, or cowardly manner, but that I will protect such from evil and danger so far as I can, and promote, to the utmost of my ability, their present welfare and eternal salvation.

[6] The 1890 version, current for General Booth, when writing, reads: I do here declare that I will spend all the time, strength, money, and influence I can in supporting and carrying on this War, and that I will endeavor to lead my family, friends, neighbors, and all others whom I can influence, to do the same, believing that the sure and only way to remedy all the evils in the world is by bringing men to submit themselves to the government of the Lord Jesus Christ.

[7] The 1890 version, current for General Booth, when writing, reads: I do here declare that I will always obey the lawful orders of my Officers, and that I will carry out to the utmost of my power all the Orders and Regulations of the Army; and further, that I will be an example of faithfulness to its principles, advance to the utmost of my ability its operations, and never allow, where I can prevent it, any injury to its interests or hindrance to its success.

[8] The 1890 version, current for General Booth, when writing, reads: And I do here and now call upon all present to witness that I enter into this undertaking and sign these Articles of War of my own free will, feeling that the love of Christ who died to save me requires from me this devotion of my life to His service for the Salvation of the whole world, and therefore wish now to be enrolled as a Soldier of the Salvation Army.

PART 2 | Section 1

Old Declarations.

Full Determination

"Therefore, I do here and now, and forever, renounce the world with all its sinful pleasures, companionships, treasures, and objects, and declare my full determination boldly to show myself a soldier of Jesus Christ in all places and companies, no matter what I may have to suffer, do or lose by so doing."

1. What is the premise of this first declaration?

God's character is such that what He commands, He enables (that is, He is not a mean-spirited God commanding the impossible so He can punish us for failing to live up to it). He is benevolent—He shows goodwill. And so, our understanding of holiness is reflected in intention and not performance. The argument for legalism in the Articles of War is plausible but falls when we recognize that the focus is intention instead of performance.

2. You mention holiness. What does holiness have to do with it?

This declaration separates us from casual Christians who disgrace the Holy Spirit, intentionally or not, by declaring that they sin every day. How can God trust someone who intends to sin every day? How can you trust such a person at your shoulder when you go to war? No, I am going to trust a covenanted warrior who declares a full determination boldly to show himself or herself a soldier of Jesus Christ in all places and companies, no matter what he or she may have to suffer, do or lose by so doing (see 2 Timothy 2:3,4).

Reading Club Guide

How are we tempted to fall into the legalistic trap of performance instead of intention?

How can we protect ourselves and our comrades from this danger?

Do you agree with this declaration? If not, how can you align yourself with it?

PART 2 | Section 2

Total Abstinence.

"I do here and now declare that I will abstain from the use of all intoxicating liquor, and from the use of all baneful drugs, except when such drugs shall be ordered for me by a doctor."

1. Where is the grace in this declaration?

I know that this is the one that gets the "grace" crowd all riled up.[1]

I'm not exactly sure what the big deal is about. I don't want my sons drinking alcohol or taking drugs. And I'll have them promise me not to do it. I won't settle for something like this: "Father, I'm not going to drink very much alcohol," or "Daddy, I won't drink any beer but I might do the occasional drug." I'm going to expect them not to drink and not to do drugs. I see no debate on this one at all.

If they keep their promise I can trust them. If they don't, I can't *(see Judges 13-16)*.

From a long-term perspective—I'm talking six or seven thousand years—arguments to allow breach of covenant in favor of "relevance" or "relationship" are paltry, petty, and preposterous.

2. What, then, are the benefits of this declaration?

Covenanted people are widely admired and generally outstanding in their effect. You can depend on covenanted people to act in certain ways. Here are some popular examples from cinema:

Group	Context	Characteristics
Samurai	Last Samurai movie	sacrifice, simplicity ...
Jedi	Star Wars series	set apart, disciplined, loyal
Scots	Braveheart movie	citizenship, belonging
Myrmidons	Troy movie	training, loyalty
Freedom Fighters	Matrix series	sacrifice, revelation[2]

It is also the nature of an army. You can't be in it unless you commit. And if you don't commit, you can't be counted on in battle. All the more does this apply in the spiritual warfare in which The Salvation Army engages.

Reading Club Guide

Are you part of "the grace" crowd on this issue?
If so, how do you respond?

How can Salvationist covenant benefit us (spinning off the movie list above or your own customized movie list)?

---

[1] The "grace" crowd seems to misunderstand antinomianism as grace such that "grace" for them might be akin to what Bonhoeffer identified as "cheap grace."

[2] Movies for the following two groups are yet to be produced:

The 30	David	heroic
Death and Glory	Booth-Tucker	elite troops

PART 2 | Section 3

Words Have Power.

"I do here and now declare that I will abstain from the use of all low or profane language and from all impurity, including unclean conversation, the reading of any obscene book or paper at any time, in any company, or in any place."

1. To what extent is this merely a determination to impose a discipline on your tongue?

It is not a matter of internally tightening the cranks and bolting the lips to protect yourself from breaking this promise. This is a natural fruit of integrity in your life. It is a supernatural fruit of the Holy Spirit filling your life.

2. Doesn't Scripture suggest that it is a severe self-imposition of discipline?

No. Ephesians 4:29 instructs, "Don't let any unwholesome word come out of your mouth but only what is profitable for building up, as there is need, so that your words may give grace to those who hear."[1]

This instruction flows out of a long grocery list of social instructions from Paul. You might infer that it is, then, a matter of taping your lips shut and toughening it up. But the whole section in chapter 4 begins with "Therefore." And Paul is building on his famous apostolic prayer for these people, that,

> According to the riches of His glory, He may grant that you may be strengthened in your inner being with power through His Spirit, and that Christ may dwell in your hearts through faith, as you are being rooted and grounded in love. I pray that you may have the power to comprehend, with all the saints, what is the breadth and length and height and depth, and to know the love of Christ that surpasses knowledge, so that you may be filled with all the fullness of God. Now to Him who, by the power at work within us, is able to accomplish abundantly far more than all we can ask or imagine, to Him be glory in the church and in Christ Jesus to all generations, forever and ever. Amen. *(Ephesians 3:16-20)*

Once we get rooted and grounded in love and filled with the fullness of God, then it is natural that we, "abstain from the use of all low or profane language and from all impurity, including unclean conversation, the reading of any obscene book or paper at any time, in any company, or in any place."

3. Isn't reading obscenity a hidden problem, even for Christians?

Jesus was tempted as we are, in every way. If He had speedy internet He'd probably run across some of the devil's stupid options for flirtatious and pornographic sites and pictures. This is possibly the most insidious temptation for a lot of Christians, because it is private. So, don't be stupid about your internet use. I know guys who have totally messed up on this point.[2] Don't put yourself in position to be messed up if that is an issue for you.

The better response, though, emerges from that same apostolic prayer: Get to know the breadth and length and height and depth of the love of Christ so that the temptation is removed.

This is an important issue. We want to be a pure and spotless bride decked out in Army boots that we use to stomp all over the devil's jugular. That means we need total purity, in our conversation, innuendo, and our language.

4. As difficult as you make these things out to be, why promise it? Why not just aim for it?

Why promise it? We're stepping apart. We're putting ourselves on the line. We're positioning ourselves so that God can trust us with His power. We're not going to try. We're going to take God at His word and, by His power, actually obey.[3]

Reading Club Guide

What are some ways that we unintentionally curse people and speak death over them?

How has self-imposition of discipline on this issue failed for you in the past? How can holiness change the outcome this time around?

How can we establish accountability regarding issues like pornography in our own lives?

---

[1] My buddy Peter Thackwray often quotes this verse and always models it. Hallelujah.

[2] And I'm told that women are not immune. General Paul Rader is on the board of Pure Hope - http://purehope.net—which is aiming to help people overcome this addiction.

[3] One of the best ways we've found to help us along in discipleship and accountability is the new rule of life called Infinitum (Latin for Boundless—key word in that famous song Booth made up, O Boundless Salvation!), composed of one vision, two virtues, and three vows:

Vision: follow Jesus;

Virtues: loving God, loving others;

Vows: Surrender, Generosity, Mission.

For more information and to register with Infinitum, see Infinitumlife.com.

PART 2 | Section 4

Dealing Honorably.

"I do here declare that I will not allow myself in any deceit or dishonesty; nor will I practice any fraudulent conduct in my business, my home or in any other relation in which I may stand to my fellow men; but that I will deal truthfully, honorably and kindly with all those who employ me or whom I may myself employ."

1. What do you make of this declaration?

Again, this is basic Christian stuff. I wouldn't want to hire anyone who couldn't sign this statement. Neither would I want to work alongside or live with such a person. These are basic statements for people with the guts to put their word on the line and promise God in such a way that He can count on us to fulfill the promises.

2. What are the disadvantages of such a policy?

Whatever they are, the disadvantages are short-term. Any advantage you might gain at the expense of your honor, truthfulness, or kindness, is not worth it. Among other things it accelerates the decay of those virtues in your life.

3. What are the advantages of living by this promise?

Besides the pleasure of God, the favor of people, and the ability to sleep at night? Well, though not the purpose, I expect that adherence to this declaration will help you win friends and influence people and be trusted with responsibility and the compensation that often accompanies it. It is Biblical that the leader's spiritual experience seems to overflow to the rest of the family *(see Leviticus 16:6; Job 1:10; Acts 16:31; Acts 18:8; etc.)*.

Reading Club Guide

Do you agree that this is basic Christian stuff you'd expect from people with whom you live and work? Discuss.

How can we fulfill this declaration in a way that intentionally blesses those around us?

PART 2 | Section 5

Protective Justice.

"I do here declare that I will never treat any woman, child or other person, whose life, comfort or happiness may be placed within my power, in an oppressive, cruel or cowardly manner; but that I will protect such from evil and danger so far as I can, and promote, to the utmost of my ability, their present welfare and eternal Salvation."

1. How does this declaration fit into 21st century society?

This is probably a good example of why there is a newer version of the Articles of War declarations that we'll tackle in the next chapter. It reads a little patriarchal. Again, though, it goes beyond being a good person or a good parent or a good employer and redefines that concept as people who are doing everything they can to get those under their influence saved and blessed while on earth.

A while ago it was vogue to call the Army a church with a plus (the idea being that we don't just worship on Sundays, but, ideally, we live it out in measurable—read social services and justice—ways through the week).[1] In a similar way soldiers are claiming to be Christians with a plus—not merely saved by the skin of our teeth but committed to being positive difference-makers in the lives of everyone we can influence. This is courageous Christianity and I know it deters some more academic and some more casual types. It takes such covenanted commitment to win the world. Merely credentialed and casual Christianity will never make it.

2. What are the important components of this declaration?

The first is that we "Do no evil." While this may be more famous these days as the motto of Google, Paul actually coined the phrase in 2 Corinthians 13:7.[2] But this is more than a spiritual Hippocratic Oath.

3. What is the other important component?

We're doing everything we can to get everyone we can to join us on our way to heaven. This is right out of one version of the Army salute.[3] It is also the hardcore question six of the Test for Self-Examination in the Orders and Regulations for Soldiers.[4] It certainly echoes Paul's approach *(see 1 Corinthians 9:22)*.

4. What else is behind this protective justice?

There is a determination to promote, to the utmost of our ability, the present welfare of those whose life, comfort, or happiness may be placed within our power. This is a justice imperative. Our power, those of us who live in the West, extends via financial, social, political, and advocacy means, to many of the more fragile in our global village. "We work for the reform of society by alleviating poverty, deprivation, and disadvantage, and by challenging evil, injustice, and oppression, in the name of Jesus."[5] There are all kinds of ways to do this on your local front.[6]

Reading Club Guide

In what ways are you involved in intentionally fulfilling this justice imperative?

How can you be more effective in this initiative?

---

[1] This "church with a plus" isn't the best phrase, as it connotes what is more accurately "Biblical Church," in which justice and service are normal components, not chosen additions.

[2] I wonder if he is in line for royalties. Maybe we could collect on his behalf, being spiritual descendants and all.

[3] I'm on my way to heaven and I'm doing everything I can to get everyone I can to join me.

[4] Am I doing all in my power for the salvation of sinners? Do I feel concern about their danger and pray and work for their salvation as if they were my children?

[5] This is the mission statement of The Salvation Army's Social Policy and Parliamentary Unit in New Zealand.

[6] We recommend our books, In Darkest England and the Way Out, and Be a Hero, as two complementary strategies of fighting for mercy and justice.

PART 2 | Section 6

All I can.

"I do here declare that I will spend all the time, strength, money and influence I can in supporting and carrying on the Salvation war, and that I will endeavor to lead my family, friends, neighbors and all others whom I can influence to do the same, believing that the sure and only way to remedy all the evils in the world is by bringing men to submit themselves to the government of the Lord Jesus Christ."

1. Where do you start on a declaration like that?

Beautiful. I know of no covenant more extreme than soldiership. I know of no one more covenanted than a Salvationist. Not only are you as zealous as possible with your time and strength and influence and money but you do all you can to get everyone else you can to be as zealous as possible with their time and strength and influence and money. Plus, of course, there is a whole book called the Orders and Regulations to accompany you as you journey through your experience of covenant.

2. Are there any theological presumptions here?

It makes motivation clear. No soft and fuzzy "liberalism" here. We're aiming to bring everyone to submit themselves to Jesus Christ. Not only that, but we see all of our other efforts, as suggested in the previous declaration, such as justice, through the perspective of salvation. So, do you want to remedy all the evils of the world? Try to get everyone saved![1] This is a reworking of the assertion, "Holiness is the solution to every problem" that drives some people crazy! How does that look with regard to oppressive, tin pot dictatorships? Compel the dictator to submit to the government of the Lord Jesus Christ. How does it look regarding the spread of HIV? Persuade fornicators to submit to the government of the Lord Jesus Christ. Do you get the idea?

God help us to live up to covenant.

3. What has this declaration to do with simplicity?

Plainly, if we're investing all the time, strength, money, and influence we can in supporting and carrying on the salvation war, other interests such as may exist get less time, less strength, less money, and less influence, and, maybe, none at all.

Captain Rowan Castle has suggested stages of simplicity. Roughly put, they range from having a lot and not sharing, through an ordinary lifestyle punctuated by moderate engagement with necessities and some attention to the poor, to a radical reconsideration of what is a necessity that includes minimizing and scaling back and a big commitment to the poor (he actually has one more stage—that of owning nothing).[2]

It's quite likely that this is a simplicity stage cycle, in that we work our way down to the penultimate level (radical reconsideration) that transforms our worldview on the whole issue such that we find ourselves back at having a lot ... *(see Matthew 8:28)*.

Does that make sense? We keep cutting, and simplifying, and scaling back. Then we experience a crisis (maybe we go on a hero holiday and visit the widow and orphan in their distress[3]) that helps us to see that all our scaling back really just leaves us still having a lot and not sharing much. So, we start the stage cycle again, living more simply and investing more in the poor ....

The cycle component comes partly from those with whom we choose to associate. The simpler those people are, the more likely we are to be challenged with our status quo.[4]

4. How do you understand "All ... I can"?

When you read "all ... I can" please don't read it as "whatever I can spare in my wallet after all the bills are paid and I've enjoyed a weekend of indulgence." In this context, a tithe (ten percent) is merely the beginning *(though required—see 2 Corinthians 9:7 and Galatians 6:6,7)*.[5] For those unsure, let us clear tithing up. It isn't an Old Testament law made obsolete by the cross. It precedes the law. Abraham tithed to Melchizedek, probably a pre-incarnate image of Jesus, before there was even a people of Israel to whom the Law could be handed down!

So, tithing is the very minimum standard. Much more is expected of soldiers. And as we prove ourselves in our generosity, God can trust us with more resources to steward. Note that the Queen of Sheba presented Solomon with the largest gift in history to that point—caravans of camels carrying unprecedented quantities of spices, gold, and precious stones (1 Kings 10). And yet, at the end of her visit, she left with an even larger gift from him *(2 Chronicles 9:12)*!

We are challenged here to run through Castle's simplicity stage cycle again and again, re-assessing our lifestyle in light of the masses rushing, with very little, to hell.

5. How do Salvationists respond?

The Salvation Army established a Cab Horse Charter in 1890. General Booth asserted that a cab horse, the taxi of that era, if it fell, could count on the following help: "a shelter for the night, food for its stomach, and work allotted to it by which it can earn its corn." Booth argued that certainly men and women deserve as much as that.

Today's equivalent might be the Bovine Standard. Every cow in the European Union gets a subsidy of 2 pounds/day. It would be nice to know that three quarters of Africans living today could enjoy the same security and luxury as the Belgian cow.

6. Isn't this taking us a little off the course prescribed in this section?

Not really. If we realize that justice issues prove both a means of accomplishing our mission and a natural expression of our Christian compassion, we're more broadly endeavoring to lead everyone we can influence to submit themselves to the Lordship of Jesus Christ.

Reading Club Guide

How have we offended you in this section?

Are the arguments persuasive?

What changes for you as a result of reading this chapter?

---

[1] Of course, we cannot "remedy" evils that are demons and powers and principalities, but we'll fight destroy their works (1 John 3:8) and to neutralize the natural inclination to sin within every soul.

[2] Castle led the Revolution congregation in Adelaide, Australia, and more recently has been a thought leader regarding The Salvation Army's engagement in missional communities in Australia.

[3] This is an allusion to one of the key challenges in our (Stephen's, with Wesley Campbell) book Be a Hero: The battle for mercy and social justice.

[4] The Salvation War has privileged us to live in Christian community with slum brothers and sisters who live simply. They are a constant challenge to our lifestyle.

[5] William Booth to soldiers: "You might work out this rule on a graduated scale, beginning at the bottom with a tenth, and going on increasing as God increases .... From a tenth you can rise to an eighth, and then to a fifth, and a fourth, and even further. Make His glory your joy, your conscience, your guide, and the Salvation of men, for time and eternity, the supreme object for which you live and trade and do everything else, and you will not go astray on this subject."

PART 2 | Section 7

Lawful Orders.

"I do here declare that I will always obey the lawful orders of my officers, and that I will carry out to the utmost of my power all the orders and regulations of the Army; and, further, that I will be an example of faithfulness to its principles, advance to the utmost of my ability its operations, and never allow, where I can prevent it, any injury to its interest, or hindrance to its success."

1. Doesn't this declaration epitomize the restrictive nature of soldiership?

Not when properly understood. We've already presented some arguments about covenant, and suggested that Christian paradox applies in this situation, too *(see Mark 10:44; 1 Corinthians 9:19)*. That is, it is only in slavery that we are truly free. Now, many will argue that slavery to Christ is intended, not slavery to some officer.

Yes. But, the key word here is "lawful." We bind ourselves to obey the lawful orders of our superior officers.[1] This is the bare minimum for any soldier in any army. There is nothing immoral even possible within this promise. It is actually a guarantee of ethical action, for, the corollary also stands. We're completely free to disobey the unlawful orders of our superior officers.

To fail on either option—to obey lawful orders or exercise freedom to disobey unlawful orders—is to compromise the testimony and effectiveness of every Junior and Senior Soldier.

2. What are the dangers of this first promise?

Don't be seduced by leader "worship." Part of your loyalty to them is manifest as loyalty to The Salvation Army. Another part shows up by measuring their leadership against the Biblical standard. Part of what makes them good leaders is your excellent "followership."

3. What else jumps out of this declaration?

Obey the Orders and Regulations. The O and R are part of covenant. The Orders and Regulations are what make us the most covenanted people I know. Yes, the O and R contain some quaint bits here and there (especially the older versions). There is a section on cleanliness because the converts were rescued from such dire situations that they actually needed counsel to wash themselves. When you remember the context it makes the whole thing heroic.

4. How do the Orders and Regulations fit in?

Here's the deal on the Articles of War. There is a spiritual footnote to the left side (doctrines). It is called the Handbook of Doctrine. There is a spiritual footnote to the right side (declarations). It is called the Orders and Regulations. We are responsible for both of these in our lives. That is why we have a revolutionary commentary on them in the first place.

5. How does it look to be, "an example of faithfulness," "advance to the utmost of my ability," and, "never allow ... injury ... or hindrance"?

One way relates to "Army-bashing." It is an old SA pastime. If bank employees complained about their bank like some Salvationists complain about the Army, their bank managers (the leader) might be expected to terminate their employment. In an Army context, you might plausibly expect a CO/DC (the leader) to terminate their soldiership.

6. How else does it look?

If the last response was the negative, this one is the positive. This involves giving up the minimal standard of Salvationism in exchange for the most heroic version we can imagine. That might mean digging into some early Salvationist book or it might mean paying a little more attention to that uniformed comrade who sticks out a bit on Sundays and the days in between. We aim to model faithfulness to the principles of The Salvation Army.

It involves advancing to our utmost abilities Army operations. However, God prods you on your specific front, whether to pray or fire a huge cartridge or support or preach or serve or evangelize, do it to the utmost of your abilities.

It involves protecting the Army from injury to its interests and hindrance to its success. While this relates to the ban on Army-bashing, it also includes speaking words of life into its interests and success.

Reading Club Guide

How have you lived by less than "the most heroic standard of Salvationism"?

What will change for you so that you can embrace this covenant?

How will people notice these changes?

[1] Some debate could ensue as to what is lawful. That is not our desire here. However, it might make sense to guess that it is lawful if within the covenant as explained in the Orders and Regulations and within the bounds of Christian morality.

PART 2 | Section 8

Till I Die.

"And I do here and now call upon all present to witness that I have entered into this undertaking and sign these Articles of War of my own free will, feeling that the love of Christ, who died to save me, requires from me this devotion of my life to His service for the Salvation of the whole world, and therefore do here declare my full determination, by God's help, to be a true soldier of The Salvation Army till I die."

1. Is this even reasonable in the 21st century?

Some think it unreasonable to expect people to commit their whole lives to anything, even the Army.

"Tell it not in Gath. Proclaim it not in the streets of Ashkelon" *(2 Samuel 1:20 NIV)*.

Unreasonable? Every day nearly 30,000 children die because of preventable diseases and starvation. There are currently possibly another 5+ billion people going to hell less quickly (than the dying children). In light of this reality, should we consider it reasonable to ask for only a partial commitment of our soldiers? Maybe Thursday night and Sunday morning? Maybe for a decade or so or until a corps officer they don't like arrives—whichever comes first? Maybe until they feel that soldiership is hindering promotion opportunities? Maybe until their friendships make their covenant inconvenient? Maybe until they're tired of the pace?

The need and the potential combine to make it unreasonable to ask for anything less.

2. Isn't there a danger of "over-challenging" people in our era?

Experts seem to barter in this lie. And some leaders have been hoodwinked by it. Their weakness seems to be a desire for relevance. Jesus over-challenges His crowd as much as anybody anywhere: "If any of you wants to be My follower, you must turn from your selfish ways, take up your cross daily, and follow Me" *(Luke 9:23 NLT)*.[1]

Jesus was right, 2,000 years ago and still is today. You can't over-challenge people in this era. This is the generation of extreme sports. Why extreme? People are looking for risk and thrill. Will watered down membership options offer that? Never in a million years.

Though tragic, this is also a generation of suicide bombers. Why are people blowing themselves up? People want to throw their lives away on something they believe will make a difference. Will moderation and committee-speak political correctness offer that? Never in a million years.

This is a generation of new and exotic party drugs. Why? People are craving danger and sensation. Will mediocrity and half measures offer that? Never in a million years.

Either you provide a godly, supernatural, holy risk and thrill, an option for people to throw their lives away on something that will make a godly difference, promising danger and sensation within the Kingdom of God, or they will do it outside God's Kingdom.

3. Why else do you think we can't over-challenge them?

Early Salvationist history is one of the great romance stories of our world. God wrapped a small group of misfits in Holy Spirit-conviction, infused them with love, dressed them in prophetic garb, fitted them with a holy disdain for dignified reputation, trained them in the sacrificial cross-life, deployed them among poor people, and transformed great swaths of the world.[2]

History is splattered with examples of Salvationists living it out. But you don't have to dust off 19th century books to find them.

Around the world you can find people living romantic, heroic lives as Salvation Soldiers, sacrificing ridiculously, warring valiantly, and loving prodigally.

4. Isn't the military ethos obsolete?

Again, the experts will assert that. And sometimes the leaders get it wrong. But the grassroots suggest something else. The driving vision for the global 24/7 Prayer Movement, the best ecumenical example of Salvation Army grassroots activism in this young century, is of an Army of Holiness.[3] It is militant, aggressive, surrendered, uncompromised stuff. Heroic. Romantic. It reads like an early Salvo *War Cry* article. How can you look at something like that and go out and ask for a partial commitment?

The worst we can do now is water things down. Watering down only produces watered down soldiers. We need to beef it up. Beefing it up produces beefed up soldiers.[4] It isn't unreasonable to expect people to commit their whole lives to this cause. It is unreasonable not to call them to this commitment.

Although the current Articles of War omits the phrase, "Till I Die," the same commitment is still there, hidden in the "footnote" —the Orders and Regulations—which we're bound to follow (see previous section): Chapter XI, section 5, paragraph 3.

Reading Club Guide

Did you sign up intentionally for life?
How do you respond to these comments?

What changes when you embrace the life-long aspect of Soldier's Covenant?

How might aggressive Christianity serve our purposes in this generation?

---

[1] Of course, He does follow up with a nice promise, "Whoever loses his life for Me will save it" (Luke 9:24 NIV).

[2] As Commissioner George Scott Railton asserted, "We are revolutionists. We know that we have passed from death unto life, and we insist on the necessity of the same sweeping change in every human being. With cries of 'Death unto sin' and 'Life unto righteousness,' we go on, determined to turn the world upside down. We are not philosophers or the theorists of revolution; but its agents. Merely to recommend revolution is contemptible. We must make it." (G.S.R., compiled by John D. Waldron. Originally appeared in the Christian Mission Magazine, January 1873.)

[3] See Peter Greig's "The Vision," in Aaron White and Stephen Court, Revolution. Credo Press. 2005.

[4] This is especially profound.

PART 3 | Section 1

Current Declarations Commentary.

Growing in Grace

"I will be responsive to the Holy Spirit's work and obedient to His leading in my life, growing in grace through worship, prayer, service and the reading of the Bible."

1. How do you understand the phrase, "growing in grace"?

John Wesley popularized, for us, the term "means of grace." The first half of this declaration seems a little poetic (read "redundant") but the last half is all about the personal means of grace. Means of grace are entry points that enable us to access God's grace in our lives. This declaration implicitly outlines a Salvationist means of grace.

2. How do we keep the promise that leads off this declaration?

It is wonderful for us to covenant obedience to the Holy Spirit ("I will be responsive to the Holy Spirit's work and obedient to His leading"). But, in order to fulfill this promise, at the very least, we need to hear Him. (How can we be responsive to His leading if we can't sense how/where He leads?) At the very least it means that we must wield the only offensive weapon—sword of the Spirit (the spoken word of God).[1] That is a gigantic covenant promise for more than a million soldiers. If fulfilled we're looking at more than a million fully-functioning prophetic warriors, responsive and obedient to the Holy Spirit's work and leading.

3. How is worship a means of grace?

We commit to worship—one of the aims of worship is to grow in grace. What kind of worship warms the heart of God? A lot could be said, but a start might look like this: humble, sin-free, excellent, in combination with a heart for justice and solidarity with the poor.[2]

4. How is prayer a means of grace?

We commit to prayer. A commitment to prayer doesn't mean grace at meals and a little grocery list before bedtime. To commit to prayer is serious stuff. What does it look like? Ask yourself, "who is someone I know characterized by a commitment to prayer?" Then ask yourself what his or her commitment to prayer looks like. That is a start towards an answer.

5. How is service a means of grace?

We commit to service. For many western Salvationists that is a tough one. Many have grown up in the middle class Army that allows us to take much credit in personal social relationships for the great work of the Army even though we have been involved in slim-to-none of it ourselves. Let's determine not to take credit for SA service when we're not doing our share.

6. How is reading the Bible a means of grace?

We commit to reading the Bible. This is not your "daily bread." This is something significant and consistent, something that sets direction and maintains an even keel. We have to anchor our Wesleyan Quadrilateral[3] on Scripture, a Scripture to which we must continually give space to speak to us, training, teaching, correcting, rebuking for World Conquest *(see 2 Timothy 3:16)*.

These are Salvationist means of grace. This is how we can position ourselves downstream in the river of God's grace.

Reading Club Guide

Which of the means of grace do you use most consistently and fruitfully?

Which means is an area in which you'd like to invest more? How?

What effects will be experienced when each comrade soldier in your corps or staff member at your Salvation Army program embraces this declaration?

[1] The sword of the Spirit, in Ephesians 6, is the "rhema" of God, the spoken word of God. We need to hear God if we're going to effectively attack.

[2] By "sin-free" please see what we mean by reviewing the chapters on sanctification.

[3] The Wesleyan Quadrilateral is a balanced theological approach to important questions that considers Scripture, tradition, reason, and experience, with Scripture as the base. Paul Wesley Chilcote recounts a helpful revelation on the Quadrilateral—The Wind Chime:

In this wind chime image, Scripture, again, has central place. It is the foundation, the base, the primary source and criterion for Christian doctrine and life. But Scripture itself must be balanced by the counterweight of the chimes (tradition, reason, and experience), all of which are tied directly into the biblical witness. None of these stands, as it were, independent of Scripture or of the other norms with which each interacts. Each has its own tone, its own voice that needs to sound out for music to be made. The Scriptures actually come to life in new historical settings and cultural contexts as they are "illumined by tradition, vivified in personal experience, and confirmed by reason," as it says in the Book of Discipline (Para. 104, 77). Moreover, the music of these chimes is not produced by their collision. Rather, in most wind chimes, a clapper or ball is suspended from the very center of the base—rooted as it were in the heart of Scripture— swinging back and forth among the chimes to strike the tones. This ball is, for me, the community of faith, the church, that is involved in a dynamic way with each and all of these norms related to Christian praxis.

One final touch. The purpose of the wind chime is to make music. If there is no wind, then the chimes stand stagnant, purposeless, and silent. But when the wind blows—when a dynamic force sets the wind chime in motion—then the music begins. The wind in this image is, of course, the Holy Spirit. It is the Spirit that, as the Wesleys would say, animates the whole.

When the fresh wind of the Spirit blows, and the church struggles to deal with the issues, questions, and concerns of the day in this dynamic way, the consequence is a song. That music will sound differently, perhaps, in different times and different places because the chimes may be made of wood here, or metal there, or bamboo somewhere else. But the music comes nonetheless from our faithful interaction with God's Word. (Rethinking The Wesleyan Quadrilateral, by Paul Wesley Chilcote)

PART 3 | Section 2

Kingdom Values.

"I will make the values of the Kingdom of God and not the values of the world the standard for my life."

1. How are worldly values a temptation?

At the risk of concentrating on specks rather than logs, this promise points out a temptation amongst Christian leadership. World values and standards seem to crush in on Christian leadership. They want us to conform in our structure and style and system. They glamorize the successful Church leaders[1]. They intimidate us by their degrees and size and cash and flash. They marginalize us from most debates. They show disdain for our morals.

2. For whom else are worldly values a temptation?

Obviously, this is a great temptation for soldiers, too! Many of us wander through life, unblinkingly accepting (in western culture) that we dress with certain patches and names and logos on our apparel, that we wear certain styles and flash certain amounts of flesh, that we drink certain beverages, that we get college degrees, that we vote socially liberal, that we support saving whales and killing unborn babies, that we work protracted hours five and six days a week to rush into and through a handful of hours of relaxation every weekend, that we go into debt to get the nicest house and car and television that the bank will allow us, that promotion in our jobs is desirable, that we live to get more, and so on. That is not to say that all of these values are worldly and worthless but that in many cases we uncritically accept a package of beliefs en masse some values of which might not be priorities in Kingdom warfare or even compatible with Christian lifestyle. In some cases, it is not their presence on the list that makes them worldly but the comparative (and inflated) value that the world ascribes them.

3. How do Kingdom values contrast with worldly values?

The Kingdom's values are usually upside down *(Acts 17:6 AV)*. We dress modestly. We will drink for thirst and pleasure rather than for appearances. We care more about education than a degree (and college need not factor into that equation). We're not socially liberal. We care about saving unborn babies. We—some of us I know—are employed for as short a time as necessary to pay bills so that the rest of the time can be invested straight into the Salvation War. We try to avoid debt. We look for spiritual influence potential in a job before its title or cash flow. We live to get more saved. And so on.

4. How do you keep this promise?

It is a big promise. How do we keep it? Yes, read the Bible. Pray every day. But more than that, we need to continually challenge ourselves to ensure we haven't compromised into the shape of the world.[2] USA Central Salvationist Eric Himes has two questions we might use profitably:

> As a Christian I must be asked: "How's your relationship with the Lord?" As a Salvationist I must be asked: "How's your relationship with the poor?" Both want sincerity, not charity.

A time-honored Salvationist way of keeping the promise is to get involved in a community of radicals who are continually engaged in this struggle, who are committed to extending Kingdom values and reign throughout the world. Iron sharpens iron. One framework for this way of life, called Infinitum, is proving effective in many countries in recent years.[3]

Reading Club Guide

How can you see you and your friends keeping this promise?

How do you fight the worldly temptations?

What are the effects in your corps of a counter-cultural mindset?

---

1 We are not saying that successful Church leaders are all worldly. We are suggesting that worldly values and standards tempt us to glamorize such leaders.

2 The Test for Self-Examination in the Orders and Regulations for Soldiers (Chose to Be a Soldier) is great regular resource for challenging yourself and your accountability partners.

3 In our 2016 book Reinventing the Movement: What if Knaggs is Right? (with Joe Noland) we outline a model of streamlined Salvationism called the Base Network (bases being a North American re-branding of the popular SA operating unit called "society"). Here is the simple formula: Base = cells + hubs. You know cell groups—open groups where visitors can encounter the Gospel, the Kingdom, Christian community, and much more. Hubs are the component unit of the Infinitum (Latin for "boundless") way of life described elsewhere in this book. They are closed accountability and discipleship groups (see infinitumlife.com for more details). Bases represent streamlined Salvationism that are rapidly replicable. There—that saves you reading the whole Reinventing book! But if you are interested, you can read it free, here: http://themore-revolution.wixsite.com/reinventthemovement

PART 3 | Section 3

Utter Integrity.

"I will uphold Christian integrity in every area of my life, allowing nothing in thought, word or deed that is unworthy, unclean, untrue, profane, dishonest or immoral."

1. What does this declaration mean?

A promise to uphold integrity "in every area of (your) life" is redundancy, as to hold integrity in only some parts of your life and not in others would not be integrity but hypocrisy or dishonesty.

2. So what purpose does this declaration serve?

The rest of the promise tries to sketch out what integrity looks like—no thought, word, or deed that is sinful or unworthy.

3. What kind of promise is that?

This is a holiness promise *(see 1 Thessalonians 2:10)*. Tragically, today, in many circles, the vast majority of solid Salvationists—note, we're not talking about the slackers or pew warmers here but solid Salvationists—don't even buy that we can be holy. So, for this majority, the promise at hand must be very difficult. It requires that they organize their lives carefully, that they keep track of their thoughts and words and deeds to check, that they put a guard on their mouths, that they take their own thoughts captive, that they grit their spiritual teeth to ensure that no unclean or unworthy thought slips in and no untrue or profane word slips out.

4. Why are good Salvationists in such a predicament?

These people are keen Salvos, effective warriors, some of the cream of the Army. But some are influenced and taught outside the Army by Christians outside the holiness stream.

5. Are there any other ramifications of this problem?

Dreadfully, there is a significant minority exception to the last statement consisting of the second generation of those trained up and influenced by our own Salvationist preachers and teachers who didn't and don't believe in holiness.

6. What is the solution?

Of course, the solution for them is to sit at the feet of Jesus and Paul and John and Samuel Logan Brengle again, to neutralize the natural inclination to sin, to allow the Holy Spirit to actually fill and animate, and then not worry any longer about every breath and thought and word and deed. It actually makes the promise something less than laughably impossible. But until then, grit away.

Reading Club Guide

Are you part of the "fill and animate" school or the "grit away" club? Discuss.

How can we optimize the Army's influence on our lives and or corps?

How can we spread the message of holiness more effectively?

PART 3 | Section 4

Christian Ideals.

"I will maintain Christian ideals in all my relationships with others: my family and neighbors, my colleagues and fellow Salvationists, those to whom and for whom I am responsible, and the wider community."

1. What are we promising here?

Basically, we're reiterating the first declaration, that we will live with Christian integrity. The first one dealt with every area of my life. This one deals with every relationship in my life. We learn from repetition.

2. What strikes you about this promise?

It doesn't settle with just getting by. It aims at the very best—the "excel still more" exhortation of Paul *(1 Thessalonians 4:1)*. So, we aim not to avoid an affair, but to treat women like our kid sister (honor and protect). We aim not to avoid fornication but to avoid the appearance of evil. We aim not to bring up our kids so that they stay out of jail, but that they stay into Jesus. We aim not to merely get along with our comrades but to encourage, sharpen, and bless them. We aim not only to avoid being a negative influence in the neighborhood, but to be a supernaturally positive one.

3. Doesn't it ask too much?

Well, we just don't promise to aim at it, we promise to actually maintain Christian ideals. We're in it to accomplish and experience the very best in all of our relationships. So, we want our marriage to be the best one ever. We want to be the best parents ever. I want to be the best warrior, the best soldier, the best friend, and so on. It's entirely over-the-top, but those are the ideals.

4. How can we justify this declaration?

We go through this life once. Then we sit through eternity. We want there to be no regrets at all about any of it. This declaration charges us forward from a purely private integrity to an infectious, idealistic integrity that purifies our whole circle of influence. God, help us.

Reading Club Guide

What do you think of the assertions about this declaration? Discuss.

PART 3 | Section 5

Sanctity in the Home.

"I will uphold the sanctity of marriage and of family life."

1. Why is this promise important?

The world is quickly losing the concept of good and godly marriage and good and godly family.

2. How does a godly marriage look?

This is Australia Southern Territory's statement on marriage:

"The family unit—father, mother and children—is still the ideal social institution in contemporary Australian life.

"By marriage the family remains the basic source of nurture, of love, of economic and other life supports, of fundamental education and socialization and of spiritual and moral development...

"The Salvation Army affirms its absolute conviction that the marriage of one man to one woman is a sacred institution ordained by God and that a traditional good-faith commitment to an indissoluble union is one of the most rewarding of life's decisions for any man or woman, providing the optimal conditions for family life.

"We encourage married couples to continually seek ways to enrich their relationship and to seek counselling quickly should difficulties arise.

"We encourage parents to discover how best to develop a close relationship of mutual trust and respect with their children and to accept responsibility for their children's physical, moral and spiritual growth and well being."

3. How does a godly family look?

This is Canada and Bermuda Territory's statement on family:

"The Salvation Army believes the family, as the basic community in society, ought to be the principal way in which values and morality are nourished. In an environment of love and respect, children and adults find security and wellbeing. Here they are free to develop morally, spiritually, mentally, physically and emotionally.

"We believe that the family is ideally rooted in the Biblical concept of a marriage covenant of one man and one woman. An enduring commitment to loving care reflects God's design for family life which allows no justification for abuse.

"The Salvation Army acknowledges that families of all types struggle, and at times fail to be communities of love. In following the example of Jesus Christ, The Salvation Army seeks to strengthen marriage and enrich family life, extending appropriate ministries of a caring Christian community to all people."

4. So how does it look to uphold the sanctity of marriage and the family?

It may look like recognizing and remembering that these institutions actually are established by and devoted to God. Mutual submission honors God *(Ephesians 5:21)*.

5. How does it look for marriage devoted to God? Or a family devoted to God?

These are questions we who are married and in families ought often to ask ourselves. We expect that they are microcosmic examples of the larger family of God.

Reading Club Guide

How can we model great, godly families and marriages? Discuss.

PART 3 | Section 6

Faithful Steward.

"I will be a faithful steward of my time and gifts, my money and possessions, my body, my mind and my spirit, knowing that I am accountable to God."

1. Recognizing the earlier discussion from the previous declarations, what can be said of this?

A steward is a person who manages another's property and/or finances. As Christians, we are acknowledging and celebrating that all that we are and all that we have actually belongs to God. They are His possessions. So, in living our lives effectively, we are managing God's time and gifts, His money and possessions, His body, His mind and His spirit.

2. What else can be said?

That about says it all. None of it is ours. All of it is His. So, we have to be very careful with the whole thing.

We're accountable to God for our handling of His possessions *(see Romans 14:12)*.

Reading Club Guide

What has God entrusted you with as a steward?

How can you be more faithful with these responsibilities?

PART 3 | Section 7

Not Enslaved.

"I will abstain from alcoholic drink, tobacco, the non-medical use of addictive drugs, gambling, pornography, the occult, and all else that could enslave the body or spirit."

1. What is a benefit of this declaration?

Do you mean, besides health and savings versus delusion and bondage?

This is where we outdo the Rechabites and Nazirites *(Jeremiah 35 and Numbers 6)*. Yes, we're set apart. In a post-Christian era, brand is important—people want to know who we are, what we stand for—more than just "Christian."

We wear a uniform and don't drink or smoke or gamble or do drugs or gawk at pornographic websites or dabble in the occult and we're very visible. We're walking billboards. It is important. So, it is important to identify ourselves to people we are trying to reach.

2. What important theological point is implicit here?

There is only one slavery allowed—slavery to God, not body or spirit. And we cannot serve two masters *(Matthew 6:24)*.

Reading Club Guide

Have you served two masters?
How has that gone?

How has faithfulness to this declaration aided our witness?

How are we like the Rechabites and Nazirites?
How are we dissimilar?

PART 3 | Section 8

Faithful.

"I will be faithful to the purposes for which God raised up The Salvation Army, sharing the good news of Jesus Christ, endeavoring to win others to Him, and in His name caring for the needy and the disadvantaged."

1. Without rehashing previous arguments, what stands out here?

Some suggest that when this new version of Articles of War was created the phrase "I will" won out over "I will try." We are glad of it.

2. What is implicit in this declaration regarding history?

So, "I will be faithful to the purposes for which God raised up The Salvation Army." The wording is important. It goes to first purposes and gives no room for any possible historic distractions. What is the first purpose of The Salvation Army? To win the world for Jesus. We have more than a million soldiers covenanted to be faithful in our fight to win the world for Jesus. Powerful.

3. What is explicit in this promise?

We will be faithful in sharing the good news of Jesus Christ. So, we need to intentionally evangelize *(twice a year—in season and out of season—2 Timothy 4:2)*. I suspect that this includes a hearing heart in our normal adventures, and, also, regular, specific times of evangelizing.

4. What else is explicitly promised?

We will be faithful in endeavoring to win others to Him. This emphasizes our dissatisfaction with merely "planting seeds." We're *actually* about seeing people repent of their sins and place their lives in the control of Jesus Christ *(Mark 1:15)*. We're *actually* expecting people to accept Jesus' invitation for them to come into His life *(Mark 1:17)*. We're *actually* anticipating that they will be crucified with Christ and no longer live, allowing, instead, for Christ to live in them *(Galatians 2:20)*.

5. Is there any other explicit promise?

We will be faithful in caring for the needy and disadvantaged in Jesus' name. Hallelujah, let's faithfully care for the needy and disadvantaged. What does that look like? Well, it might look like advocacy. It might look like sharing. It might include giving and training. It could even be listening. It is those and many more things. It is a tough one, because we're talking about real lives and real problems. But let's be faithful *(Matthew 25:21)*.

Reading Club Guide

How are you currently being faithful to the purposes for which God raised up the Army?

How might your evangelism change in light of this section?

How might your service change in light of this section?

PART 3 | Section 9

Large Proportions.

"I will be actively involved, as I am able, in the life, work, worship and witness of the corps, giving as large a proportion of my income as possible to support its ministries and the worldwide work of the Army."

1. What does "as I am able" mean?

Now, "as I am able" relates to physical conditions that might keep you or me from fulfilling the rest of the promise. But it is an unfortunate phrase because it opens up an excuse for backsliders. They can just say, "I'm not able." "Able" is a tricky word in this context. It could mean, "I'm not able to worship at holiness meetings because I take my boat out on Sundays." But that abuses the intention of the declaration.

2. What about money?

We promise to fire as large a cartridge as possible. This is Luke 6:38 (NLT) today:

> Give, and you will receive. Your gift will return to you in full—pressed down, shaken together to make room for more, running over, and poured into your lap. The amount

you give will determine the amount you get back.

How much do we all fail on this one? I mean, largest possible? Government welfare in Los Angeles county provides $221 (or so) a month (for single folk). In some cases, this includes all of expenses, from room to board. That's $51/week. So, theoretically, a single person making much more than that, say $1,000/week after taxes, could fire a cartridge of $949/week. Nice. Granted, things get a little more complicated when you add children to the equation.

Now, we're not advocating that everyone lives on this much money (although if anyone in the developing world gets hold of this book I suspect they'd jump at $51/week). We're just throwing it out there because we promised to give, "as large a proportion of (our) income as possible." How much is possible? You and God decide.

3. What is the argument against this proposition?

Again, you can interpret "possible" softly like this—as large as possible:

1. within my lifestyle;

2. and still go away on an annual cruise;

3. and keep my home entertainment system up-to-date;

4. and save up for my kid's college education;

5. and save a little crazy money;

6. and see at least a movie a month;

7. and stack up my retirement savings plans to the max;

8. and put aside some cash for the kids;

etc.

4. Is that a legitimate perspective?

There is no way around this as a shockingly high expectation. It is one that should challenge us daily as we make financial decisions. The problem is that it probably doesn't really challenge too many of us, very often. This is a call to simplicity and Kingdom investment. Not one or the other. We don't live simply and give cash to lost pets or whale saving ventures. We live simply and invest the cash into the Kingdom. Neither do we make our cash and fire our tenth. That's not even close to what is happening here. No. Most of us will be positioned to follow Wesley's advice: Make all you can; save all you can; give all you have.[1]

Reading Club Guide

What is most offensive about this section?

When were you last challenged as to the size of your cartridge? Discuss.

What about that person from the developing world getting his hands on this book? What claim has he on our understanding of the words "able" and "possible"?

---

[1] We're aware that the third point ended, "give all you can" but we've read that when he actually preached it, Wesley got so stirred up he went for everything, thus, "all you have."

PART 3 | Section 10

Popularity or Persecution.

"I will be true to the principles and practices of The Salvation Army, loyal to its leaders, and I will show the spirit of Salvationism whether in times of popularity or persecution."

1. How important is this declaration?

It is probably so important that every soldier (officers included) should read that one again. Suffering isn't that popular *(see 1 Peter 1:6; 4:13,16)*. Email it to your friends, comrades, leaders, session mates, and so on, because if we all follow it, the devil will run and hide in a corner.

2. What are the principles?

This gets us into the essentials and non-negotiables debate. This is not an uninteresting discussion, but it has played out without consensus. This book asserts that the one common bond is covenant. Some Salvationists suggest it is the poor. Others agree on simplicity. That makes three right there. And none of these three is strong in the West, let alone really characteristic of the movement in this theatre of war.

The covenant bond is prescriptive rather than descriptive. A universal embrace of covenant within The Salvation Army is the most lethal weapon at our disposal. Covenant is who and what we are. Captain Rowan Castle coined the term, "collective of the covenanted."

3. What are the practices?

Our historic modus operandi is: Capture, Train, Deploy. We capture souls for Jesus. We train them up in discipleship and war-fighting. We deploy them on fronts to capture more from the enemy.[1]

4. How does loyalty to our leaders manifest?

In war, failure to obey can be fatal. In battle, pausing to question leaders can prove fatal. We recognize that God has raised up The Salvation Army. And so we pray for our leaders. We hope for them. We cheer them on (Psalm 20). And we fight for them. After all, as General Booth asserted, "without excuses and self-consideration of health, or limb, or life, true soldiers fight, live to fight, love to fight, love the thickest of the fight, and die in the midst of it." We need to be very careful in our soldiership.

5. What is the spirit of Salvationism?

The spirit of Salvationism encompasses infectious joy, love for the lost, strong faith, burning compassion, and probably more.

6. What about times of persecution?

Most in the Western world are not in a position to speak to this issue since we live in countries in which the Army is appreciated, lauded, and visible. It is easy to be true in such situations. It is probably more difficult in communist, Muslim, and poor countries. God help us be true.

Reading Club Guide

What are your views on the principles and practices of The Salvation Army? Discuss.

What are the non-negotiables?

How can covenant end the discussion?

---

[1] Our micro-MO is drill/deploy/debrief.

PART 3 | Section 11

Full Determination.

"I now call upon all present to witness that I enter into this covenant and sign these Articles of War of my own free will, convinced that the love of Christ, who died and now lives to save me, requires from me this devotion of my life to His service for the salvation of the whole world; and therefore do here declare my full determination, by God's help, to be a true soldier of The Salvation Army."

1. This has been covered already. Is there anything else noteworthy?

It is interesting to note the update from "Christ, who died to save me," to, "Christ, who died and now lives to save me." This implicitly satisfies those desiring an addition to doctrine 11 that includes something explicit about Jesus' resurrection *(see 1 Peter 3:18; Romans 6:10)*.

2. What else?

The whole exercise is completely ludicrous without the phrase "by God's help." The whole part 2 of this book is meaningless without God's help. It is all only pitiful striving and self-immolation and legalism without God's help.

But, Hallelujah, with God's help, it is a lethal weapon against the enemy's hopes and purposes.

Reading Club Guide

Based on the preceding, have you been less than a true soldier of The Salvation Army? Discuss.

What specific changes can take place so that you can be a true soldier, by God's help?

What might be the impact on the world if more than 1.6 million junior and senior soldiers become true soldiers?

Soldier's Covenant

The Articles of War that all senior soldiers now sign are known collectively as the Soldier's Covenant.

1. Why the change in name?

We're led to believe that this current name is intended to suggest some of the theological depth that might be lacking in "Articles of War."

We suspect that a concern for relevance was also a factor. But it remains as revolutionary as ever when applied with wholehearted devotion and a willing mind.

2. What is the strength of the term "Soldier's Covenant"?

It emphasizes that this pledge, this promise, is actually a binding covenant.

3. Aren't there usually two parties in a covenant?

Yes. But the Christian marriage covenant is an example of three parties: God, the bride, and the groom. In a similar way, God, The Salvation Army and the individual recruit/soldier are party to this covenant.

4. What is a covenant?

It is a binding agreement. The Hebrew word is sometimes translated alliance, solemn oath, or treaty.

5. How is it made?

Well, normally it is cut. You cut a covenant. Usually, blood is shed. Whether circumcision or Abraham's covenant with the God of Abraham *(Genesis 15)*, something bleeds. The term "covenant" emerges from Latin "con venire," or, "come together."

You might say that one can't cut a covenant without bloodshed. In fact, that is what the cutting is all about. Whether it is Abraham and God, with God mysteriously passing through chopped up animals, a junior soldier enrollment on a Sunday morning, or Jesus on the Cross, covenant always involves death.

6. Why don't we hear too much about covenant these days?

Covenant has a tough time in millennium three, during which apologetic soldiers, burdened by spiritual inferiority complex, figure that we cannot challenge anyone to sign his or her life away in covenant with God through the Army. This attitude completely misses the mystery and power of covenant.

Maybe the implied death is the reason it lacks in popularity. Who wants to die? Who wants to die to self, to comfort, to habits, to ease? Who wants to suffer?

7. What is the premise behind our covenant?

As USA Southern Captain Rob Dolby says, "You can't earn God's love, but you can earn His trust."

You see, our Father delights to give us the Kingdom *(Luke 12:32, Young's Literal Translation, etc.)*. As well as peace, righteousness, and joy in the Holy Spirit *(Romans 14:17 NBV)*, the Kingdom involves all sort of supernatural interventions. Our Father would love to delight in us by releasing the fullness of His Kingdom, if He could trust us with it. Like Elisha, after picking up the mantle, our covenant provides a holy trustworthiness that allows God to release Kingdom fullness and, in so doing, take delight in us.

Do we want the wonder-working, world-winning power of the Kingdom that God delights to give us? One of the keys is the trust generated only by covenant holiness.

8. Are there any biblical examples?

The best example is the Nazirites. Their name means "separated." Covenant sets people apart for God. These people were characterized by their holiness, their submitted, sacrificial, obedience.

9. How is your premise demonstrated in the lives of the Nazirites?

We know only a few Nazirites in the Bible, and all of them were wonder-working world-winners:

- Samson *(Judges 13)* demonstrated superhuman power in leading Israel in revolt against the Philistines. Among other things, he killed one thousand with a jawbone of a donkey.

- Samuel *(1 Samuel 1:11,28)* led Israel into its golden era, and all the while none of his words fell to the ground (that is, he was a very accurate prophet). He dragged a rag-tag collection of tribes into nationhood.

- John *(Luke 1:15)* lived a fasted, prophetic lifestyle that ushered in the way of the Lord. Not only that, but, as a good prophet, he called out the inheritance, and he destroyed the destroyer (feasting on the harvest—destroyer, the locust).

- Paul[1] *(Acts 21:23-26)* performed all kinds of miracles while spreading the Gospel throughout the known world. Paul took a truth from a hidden corner of an empire and made it into the largest religion in the world.

10. And what is the connection between their exploits and their covenant?

Might it not be that while they couldn't earn God's love, they certainly earned His trust? Might it be that their disciplined, committed, covenanted lives made their behavior dependably predictable such that God could delegate His power and authority through them?

11. But didn't Samson mess things up?

Samson's wonder-working, world-winning power came out of covenant with God. His loss of power came out of breach of covenant with God. When he compromised his intimate loyalty to God, forfeiting his holy covenant, he gave up his power. It was only as he renewed covenant, as his hair began to grow, that his power returned.

Could it be that The Salvation Army finds itself in a similar position to Samson's? Could it be that we once experienced God's wonder-working, world-winning power derived from our covenant with God but that we have lost it when we lost our way with covenant?[2]

If so, we can take heart from the verse that says, "But before long his hair began to grow back" *(Judges 16:22 NLT)*, knowing that when it did, he accomplished more in one battle than in his whole life to that point.

12. Is covenant a secondary subject when dealing with God?

God is a covenant-keeping God. If we don't understand covenant, we don't truly understand God. Throughout history God has used covenant to "bind" Himself to His people in solemn agreement. Here are a few keys examples:

Genesis 9:9-17	with Noah and a rainbow;
Genesis 15:18	with Abraham and descendants;
Exodus 19:5; 24:7-8; 34:10,27-28	with Israel at Sinai;

2 Samuel 7;	1 Chronicles 17; Psalms 89:3, etc. with David for an everlasting kingdom...

13. Are there any other notable covenanted people in Scripture?

Sure, there are David's Mighty Men, known as The Thirty *(1 Chronicles 12:18)*. There are the Rechabites *(Jeremiah 35)*. There are David and Jonathan *(1 Samuel 20)*. And so on.

There is one infamous, "group of Jews (who) got together and bound themselves with an oath to neither eat nor drink until they had killed Paul" *(Acts 23:12 NLT)*. Strangely, we don't hear anything more about them.[3]

14. Of what other value is covenant to the Salvationist?

General Booth argues that covenant is essential, "not only for those who do wrong, but to prevent people from going wrong."[4]

We've watered down our end of the covenant so much that soldiership has meant, in some cases, signing a piece of paper and going to a Saturday seminar so that you can join the band. But the Articles of War covenant is intended to provide a means to holiness. The Junior Soldier's Covenant and the Officer's Covenant have the same purpose. And this puts reins on good intentions to accomplish great ends.

15. What are the stakes?

Listen to the Army Mother, Catherine Booth:

> Let me remind you—and it makes my own soul almost reel to think of it—that God holds us responsible. He holds you responsible for all the good you might do if you had (the power of the Holy Spirit). Do not deceive yourself. He will have the five talents and their increase ... Where are the souls you might have saved? Where are the children I would have given you? Where is the fruit?[5]

16. Where do we go from here?

The potency of restored covenant is powerful beyond our comprehension. When we are living a sacrificed, committed lifestyle we have access to the promises of God. And the Gospel paradox, that only in slavery is there true freedom, liberates us to incite holy revolution around the world.

17. So, what does covenant bring Salvationists?

For Nazirites, covenant brought purity and power. For Rechabites, covenant provided fidelity, loyalty, mobility, integrity, and a jealousy for the holiness of God. For Salvationists, it reins reckless enthusiasm for mission. That is our distinctive.

Watch this. Human enthusiasm takes us only so far. It peters out within a generation, and for most, after a busy weekend! The wild and outrageous doings of primitive Salvationists would be relegated to history's footnote if they were but the humanly enthusiastic celebrations of human activity.

> If when slaves find freedom, and tradesmen make fortunes, and kindred, or friends, or neighbors are delivered from some threatened calamity, it is allowable to go mad with joy and to express it by hiring music, and beating drums, and letting off fireworks, and shouting till hoarse, and everybody says that is all right, then by the same rule, if you please, and whether please or no, we are the slaves who now have our freedom, the people who have made our fortune, we are the men who have seen our kindred and friends and neighbors saved from damnation; and therefore, we have a right to be merry.[6]

As General William Booth explains here, our antics weren't mere human enthusiasm. They were inspired by holy influence on our lives.

Now, covenant reins that enthusiasm. It purifies enthusiasm from carnality. And it steers it right at our world-winning mission. That is the power of covenant.

18. What is the danger?

Covenant holiness can provide the trustworthiness required for God to pour out the fullness of His Kingdom. There is a Spiritless covenant that brings neither holiness nor power. General William Booth exposes that danger:

> Rules and regulations are no use in themselves *apart from the man*. If we could keep you all like volcanoes in a perpetual state of eruption, we might dispense with them altogether. In heaven, I suppose there will be no commandments.... There will be no need for them. But

here they are necessary, not only for those who do wrong, but to prevent people from going wrong. They are like the lines upon which a train runs, like water upon which a streamer floats. Think of trying to drag a steamer from Glasgow to London across the land! But put it on the water and it will come easily through.[7]

Reading Club Guide

How has your understanding changed based on this chapter?

How does that affect your soldiership?

---

[1] We're aware that not everyone buys that Paul was a Nazirite. But heaps of scholars figure that he was (including Matthew Henry, Keil and Delitzsch, Expositors Bible Commentary, Barnes Notes, Wycliffe Bible Commentary ....).

[2] When we stopped embracing covenant and started emphasizing membership, when we stopped fighting the war and started explaining away our peculiar terminology and traditions, when we stopped looking solely to our God and started looking with at least one eye peeking at the green grass over the fence—this could be the season when we lost our way on covenant.

[3] They are notable to us, because God takes covenant seriously, even if we don't. The classic example in Scripture of this is Joshua's covenant with the Hivites of Gibeon in which he looks to the victuals and not to the Lord (Joshua 9:14). Generations later, Saul almost wiped this people out. Much later, David wonders why they were suffering a three-year famine. Yahweh answers, "The famine has come because Saul and his family are guilty of murdering the Gibeonites" (2 Samuel 21:1ff NLT).

[4] William Booth, "Staff Council Notes," The Officer. March, 2003.

[5] Catherine Booth, Papers on Aggressive Christianity. 1892. p. 191.

[6] William Booth, Salvation Soldiery.

[7] William Booth, "Staff Council Notes," The Officer. March 2003.

Exhortation

As we reposition ourselves downstream in the river of God's grace, we eagerly pray for the day when God unleashes the wonder-working, world-winning goodness and miracles that He has promised as part of His "Greater Things" end-time package *(John 14:12)*. General William Booth felt the same way, when he exhorted us, "By all means let us aspire after higher gifts."[1]

But even more, let us aspire after a Father who is free to delight in us because He can trust us.

It may be that we are akin to the people of Israel on the verge of entering the Promised Land. We've enjoyed the blessings of our heritage. But we've not proven trustworthy to receive the promised blessings ourselves. Those people had to enter into their own covenant with God, being circumcised after crossing the Jordan *(Joshua 5:3)*. Maybe we, too, need to take seriously holy covenant ourselves to establish a trust relationship with God that allows Him to delight in us and unleash through us the fullness of His Kingdom with wonder-working, world-winning power.

We are on the verge of global spiritual revolution.

A universal embrace of Soldier's Covenant may be the means of avoiding the potential fragmentation of The Salvation Army while simultaneously being the means of posturing ourselves so that Catherine Booth's prophecy can be fulfilled:

> The decree has gone forth that the kingdoms of this world shall become the kingdom of our Lord and of His Christ, and that He shall reign, whose right it is, from the River

to the ends of the earth. We shall win. It is only a question of time. I believe that this Movement is to inaugurate the great final conquest of our Lord Jesus Christ.[2]

Reading Club Guide

Universal embrace of covenant?
What role can you play in that? Discuss.

How can we pray toward the fulfillment of this prophecy?

What's next? Discuss.

---

1 The War Cry. March 14, 1885.

2 The War Cry (UK). February 21, 1880, p. 1. The context was her farewell to George Scott Railton and the Hallelujah Lasses (Alice Coleman, Rachel Evans, Emma Elizabeth Florence Morris, Elizabeth Pearson, Clara Price, Annie Shaw, and Emma Westbrook) deploying to invade America.

Author Resources

William Booth

William Booth wrote voluminously and influentially, including these titles:

Purity of Heart

In Darkest England and the Way Out

How to Preach

Salvation Soldiery

Sergeant-Major Do-Your-Best

The Seven Spirits

Religion for Every Day

Training of Children

Visions

Stephen Court

Stephen blogs at Armybarmy –

http://www.armybarmy.com/blog.html

He tweets here – @StephenCourt

He has these books available:

Reinventing The Movement: What if Knaggs is Right? (With Joe Noland)

Holy! Nine Lies, Half-Truths, and Outrageous Misconceptions about the Most Radical Experience You've Never Lived! (With Peter Brookshaw)

Charge! Looking Back, Facing Forward—Five Wise Words of Counsel (With Joe Noland)

Salvationism 101 (With Danielle Strickland)

All for One (The One Trilogy of Books—One Day; One Thing; One Army) (With Jim Knaggs)

The Uprising: A Holy Revolution? (With Olivia Munn)

Holiness Incorporated: Living and Working Beyond Corporate Integrity (With Geoff Webb and Rowan Castle)

Boston Common: Salvationist Perspectives on Holiness (Editor)

Proverbial Leadership: Ancient Wisdom for Tomorrow's Endeavors (With Wesley Harris)

Revolution (With Aaron White)

Be a Hero: The Battle for Mercy and Social Justice (With Wesley Campbell)

Hallmarks of The Salvation Army (With Henry Gariepy)

Greater Things: 41 Days of Miracles (With James Thompson)

High Counsel: Jesus and John on Leadership (With Joe Noland)

A Field For Exploits: Training Leaders For The Salvation Army (With Eva Burrows)

Army on Its Knees: Dynamics of Great Commission Prayer (With Janet Munn)

Boundless: Living Life in Overflow (With Danielle Strickland)

Tsunami of the Spirit: Come Roll Over Me (With Joe Noland)

Blood and Fireworks (With Xander Coleman)

To Seize this Day of Salvation (Editor, By Paul Rader With Kay Rader)

Warfare Prayer: Praying the Bible on The Battlefield of Salvation Life (With Janet Munn)

Leading the War: Officership as Vocational Extremism (With Jim Knaggs)